The Protocol Additional to the Geneva Conventions for the Protection of Victims of International Armed Conflicts and the United Nations Convention on the Law of the Sea: Repercussions on the Law of Naval Warfare

VERÖFFENTLICHUNGEN
DES INSTITUTS FÜR INTERNATIONALES RECHT
AN DER UNIVERSITÄT KIEL

Herausgegeben von

Jost Delbrück · Wilfried Fiedler
Wilhelm A. Kewenig · Rüdiger Wolfrum

90

The Protocol Additional to the Geneva Conventions for the Protection of Victims of International Armed Conflicts and the United Nations Convention on the Law of the Sea: Repercussions on the Law of Naval Warfare

Report

to the Committee for the Protection of Human Life
in Armed Conflict of the International Society
for Military Law and Law of War

by

Dr. iur. Elmar Rauch LL.M.

DUNCKER & HUMBLOT / BERLIN

CIP-Kurztitelaufnahme der Deutschen Bibliothek

Rauch, Elmar:
The protocol additional to the Geneva conventions for the protection of victims of international armed conflicts and the United Nations convention on the law of the sea: repercussions on the law of naval warfare: report to the Committee for the Protection of Human Life in Armed Conflict of the Internat. Soc. for Military Law and Law of War / by Elmar Rauch. — Berlin: Duncker und Humblot, 1984.
(Veröffentlichungen des Instituts für Internationales Recht an der Universität Kiel; 90)
ISBN 3-428-05703-1

NE: Institut für Internationales Recht ⟨Kiel⟩: Veröffentlichungen des Instituts ...

Gedruckt 1984 bei Berliner Buchdruckerei Union GmbH., Berlin 61
Printed in Germany

ISBN 3-428-05703-1

Prefatory Note

The Bureau of the International Society of Military Law and Law of War, during its meeting in The Hague (24—27 March 1983), recommended that the next International Congress take place in Garmisch-Partenkirchen and that the Committee for the Protection of Human Life in Armed Conflict inscribe the Law of the Sea and the Law of Naval Warfare on its agenda. The Board of Directors of the Society unanimously approved these recommendations at the meeting in Dublin (30 June — 3 July 1983).

Scholarly preparation of the Congress should commence early in order to enable all interested participants to familiarize themselves with the problems to be discussed. I submit this paper with the desire of contributing to the scientific success of the first International Congress of Military Law and Law of War to be held on German soil. The views expressed herein embody only my own personal reflections and should not be taken as the official position of the German Government or the Ministry of Defense. Neither, of course, do these views necessarily represent the position of the International Society for Military Law and Law of War or the Committee for the Protection of Human Life in Armed Conflict.

With the conclusion of the CDDH and UNCLOS III, the Law of Naval Warfare is a particularly suitable subject for an enlightening exchange of views within the framework of an international congress devoted to the Law of War.

Table of Contents

Abbreviations

AFDI	=	Annuaire Française de Droit International
AJIL	=	American Journal of International Law
BGBl	=	Bundesgesetzblatt
BYIL	=	British Yearbook of International Law
CCD	=	Conference of the Committee on Disarmament
CDDH	=	Diplomatic Conference on the Reaffirmation and Development of International Humanitarian Law applicable in Armed Conflicts
DEIS	=	US Navy Draft Environmental Impact Statement
DJZ	=	Deutsche Juristenzeitung
DRK	=	Deutsches Rotes Kreuz
EEZ	=	Exclusive Economic Zone
GYIL	=	German Yearbook of International Law
ICJ	=	International Court of Justice
ICRC	=	International Committee of the Red Cross
ILC	=	International Law Commission
ILM	=	International Legal Materials
LNTS	=	League of Nations Treaty Series
LOS	=	Law of the Sea
MPB	=	Marine Pollution Bulletin
PCIJ	=	Permanent Court of International Justice
RdC	=	Recueil des Cours (of the Academy for International Law, The Hague)
RDPMDG	=	Revue de Droit Pénal Militaire et de Droit de la Guerre
RGBl	=	Reichsgesetzblatt
RGDIP	=	Revue Générale de Droit International Public
SIPRI	=	Stockholm International Peace Research Institute
UN	=	United Nations
UNCLOS	=	United Nations Conference on the Law of the Sea
UNLS	=	United Nations Legislative Series
UNTS	=	United Nations Treaty Series
USNIP	=	United States Naval Institute Proceedings
USTS	=	United States Treaty Series
YILC	=	Yearbook of the International Law Commission
ZaöRV	=	Zeitschrift für ausländisches öffentliches Recht und Völkerrecht
ZVR	=	Zeitschrift für Völkerrecht

I. Introduction

With the exception of the Seabed Arms Control Treaty of 1971,[1] which in any event primarily is an arms control treaty rather than a treaty on naval warfare, the most recent instrument governing the conduct of naval warfare is almost half a century old. Even this instrument, the London Protocol of 1936 relating to restrictions on submarine warfare,[2] proved to be a dead letter during World War II. Its provisions were so completely disregarded by all belligerents that despite the irrefutable evidence, even the International Military Tribunal at Nuremberg refused to hand down a sentence against the two German admirals who had built, trained and commanded the German U-boat arm.[3]

In his 1952 article "The Problem of the Revision of the Law of War", Professor *Hersch Lauterpacht* rightly deplored the vanishing of certain aspects of the law of naval warfare, which had drawn their strength from the traditional distinction between combatants and non-combatants, military objectives and civilian objects, military needs and civilian needs. With respect to the law of contraband, the law of blockade, and the rules relating to attacks upon merchant vessels on the high seas, *Lauterpacht* wrote: "If the practice followed by both sides to the conflict is evidence of the legal position, then the traditional law on the subject, derived as it was from the notion of a legally relevant distinction between military and civilian needs, no longer exists ... In view of this there can be no question here of legal arguments drawn from the obsolete armoury of the past. The possibility must be envisaged that total war has irrevocably removed the foundations of a substantial part of this branch of the law and that juristic — or even political — efforts to give them a new lease of life may be in vain."[4] *Lauterpacht's* treatise is remarkably balanced for an Anglo-Saxon scholar, because the evaluation includes the law of contraband and the law of blockade. He thus avoids any one-sided indictment focussing exclusively on the naval operations of the Axis Powers during World War II.

---

[1] *Joachim Hinz/Elmar Rauch*, Kriegsvölkerrecht, 3rd ed., Köln/Berlin/Bonn/München 1984, No. 1514; BGBl 1972 II, 38.

[2] LNTS vol. 173 (1936—1937), 353; *Hinz/Rauch* (note 1), No. 1532.

[3] See, Judgment of the International Military Tribunal (Nuremberg) of 1 October 1946, AJIL vol. 41 (1947), 172—333 (304, 305, 308).

[4] BYIL vol. XXIX (1952), 360—382.

What *Hersch Lauterpacht* could not imagine seven years after the end of World War II has actually happened 25 years later. On 10 June 1977 the Diplomatic Conference on the Reaffirmation and Development of International Humanitarian Law applicable in Armed Conflicts (CDDH) adopted a Protocol Additional to the Geneva Conventions of 12 August 1949 and relating to the Protection of Victims of International Armed Conflicts (Protocol I).[5] As far as the combat provisions of this new treaty instrument are concerned, the basic cornerstone is precisely the revival of the distinction between civilians and combatants, civilian objects and military objectives. The examination of the effects of this new instrument on the law of naval warfare will be the focal point of this paper. Unfortunately, this is a rather difficult task precisely because of the chaotic status of the law of naval warfare which has prevailed since World War I.

Apart from some isolated cases decided during the Crimean War, the American Civil War, and the Russo-Japanese War, the law of naval warfare, including the law of prize, was a set of rules which had developed through the centuries up to the Napoleonic wars. The Declaration of Paris, signed 16 April 1856,[6] as well as the six Conventions on the Law of Naval Warfare and on the Law of Neutrality in Naval War, adopted at the Second Hague Peace Conference on 18 October 1907,[7] and the Declaration of London concerning the Law of Maritime War, signed 26 February 1909,[8] were all codifications of customary rules which had developed during the era of sail. At the outbreak of hostilities in 1914, all parties to the conflict encountered the same difficulties, namely that the traditional rules of naval warfare had become unrealistic. The introduction of new methods and means of warfare and new ways of international communication and transport had brought about tremendous changes of kind. All belligerents in the „Great War" tried more or less faithfully to adapt the generally recognized rules of law to the new circumstances they were facing. As will be shown in detail later, the Entente Powers gradually did away with the customary rules on contraband control and blockade, while the Central Powers pondered the question of which traditional rules were applicable to their highly effective new weapon, the submarine torpedo

---

[5] The text of Protocol I is reproduced in *Hinz/Rauch* (note 1), No. 1570; AJIL vol. 72 (1978), 457—502; ILM vol. 16 (1977), 1391—1441; ZaöRV vol. 38 (1978), 86—146.

[6] *Hinz/Rauch* (note 1), No. 1525; Preußische Gesetzessammlung 1856, 585.

[7] *Hinz/Rauch* (note 1), Nos. 1526—1530, 1537; RGBl 1910, 181 *et seq.*

[8] *Hinz/Rauch* (note 1), No. 1531. The authentic English text of the London Declaration of 1909 along with extremely interesting *travaux préparatoires* is published in: *James Brown Scott* (ed.), The Declaration of London, February 26, 1909, Oxford 1919.

boat. In each instance the belligerents decided in favour of what they considered to be military necessity. The Entente Powers felt justified to abolish the distinction between absolute and conditional contraband and to introduce the so-called long distance blockade in order to starve the civilian population of the enemy. The Central Powers, by the same token, considered the submarine, which had no facilities for the accommodation of crews and passengers of enemy merchant ships or neutral blockade runners, as a completely new weapon; commanders were consequently considered not subject to the rules designed for surface ships and could attack and destroy vessels in a duly proclaimed war zone without warning and without making provision for the survival of crews and passengers. Both approaches were tantamount to a complete disregard for any distinction between civilians and combatants. The ambiguity of the law under these circumstances provided an excellent opportunity for reciprocal propaganda and reprisals.

Aside from propaganda and politics, the treatment of foodstuffs as unconditional contraband and the establishment of long-distance blockades by the Entente Powers on the one hand, and the unrestricted submarine warfare waged by the Central Powers on the other created serious legal problems. Had these real-world legal problems been comprehensively analyzed, both by scholars and politicians, in the post-war-era, a significant contribution might have been made to the progressive development in the law of naval warfare; this opportunity was nevertheless wasted. The victorious Entente Powers had so successfully availed themselves of the ambiguities and grey areas of the law of naval warfare to justify their own actions that they were not interested at all in a reaffirmation and development of the pertinent rules. What they were interested in was only to outlaw the effective use of the one and only new means of naval warfare that had been used to the advantage of the Central Powers, *i. e.* the submarine. The first agreement for this purpose was the Washington Naval Treaty, signed 6 February 1922,[9] which contained stringent restrictions on the employment of submarines in naval warfare so as to prevent their use as commerce destroyers. This treaty never entered into force. The next step was the London Naval Treaty of 22 April 1930,[10] which included further restrictions on the use of submarines. These latter restrictions were subsequently incorporated into the London Protocol of 6 November 1936, mentioned above.[11]

---

[9] United States of America, Statutes at Large vol. 46, No. 2858; USTS, No. 830, Washington 1931.

[10] British Parliamentary Papers (1930), Command Paper 3758.

[11] See, *supra*, note 2.

As for the rest of the law of naval warfare, the uncertainties remained. Even with respect to the subject matter contained in the London Protocol of 1936, nothing was achieved concerning the actual conduct of combat at sea. It is my considered opinion that the chaotic status of the law of naval warfare before and during World War II is mainly due to this schizophrenic attitude of the victorious powers of World War I. If the community of nations had been genuinely interested in closing the gap between the traditional rules conceived more than a century before and the realities of war at sea in the first half of the twentieth century, the efforts would have had to extend to the law of contraband and blockade as well, rather than being restricted to the law of submarine warfare.[12]

As for World War II, one can safely say that all parties to the conflict contributed further to the erosion of the distinction which is the hallmark of Protocol I. The traditional law, founded firmly on the notion of a legally relevant distinction between military and civilian needs, was more or less wiped out.

When the International Law Commission (ILC) of the United Nations in 1949 decided on its programme of work for the following years, it considered whether the law of war should be selected as a topic for codification.[13] The majority of the ILC declared itself opposed to the study of this problem at that stage. It was suggested that if the Commission, at the very beginning of its work, were to undertake such a study, public opinion might interpret its action as a sign of lack of confidence in the efficacy of the means at the disposal of the UN for maintaining peace.[14]

More than three decades later, it is still of interest to review briefly the arguments of those opposed to including this topic on the ILC agenda. *Mr. Scelle* (France) pointed out for example, that since the Charter had outlawed war, there would no longer be any question of the law of war. *Mr. Koretsky* (USSR) argued that the Commission should not transform itself into a legal general staff, which might pursue its activities in concert with the general staff of NATO; the ILC should therefore categorically refuse to discuss war. *Mr. Brierly* (United King-

---

[12] A typical example for this legal schizophrenia can be found in the article by *H. W. Malkin*, Blockade in Modern Conditions, in: BYIL vol. 3 (1922—23), 87—98 (87), which reads in part as follows: "As to the illegality of the methods adopted by Germany, there is nothing more to be said, *securus iudicat orbis terrarum*; but as to the legality of the methods adopted by the Allies, so far as they did not fall within universally admitted rules as to contraband and blockade, there is more difference of opinion ..."

[13] YILC 1949, 51.

[14] *Op. cit.*, 281.

dom) supported *Mr. Koretsky's* remarks, although for different reasons. The Commission, he maintained, should refrain from taking up the question of the law of war, because if it did so, its action might be interpreted as a lack of confidence in the UN and the work of peace which the latter was called upon to carry out; nothing would create a worse impression of the Commission's work, nothing would upset public opinion more. Jurists, he continued, should neither study new methods of warfare, which developed with amazing rapidity, nor regulate the use of various weapons of war. *Sir Rau* (India) shared the opinions expressed by *Mr. Koretsky* and *Mr. Brierly:* The codification of the law of war at the existing time could not fail but have a deplorable psychological effect on world opinion. *Mr. Yepes* (Colombia) thought that the outlawing of war by the UN Charter rendered it a state of international anarchy for which rules could not be established. It would therefore certainly create an unfortunate impression on public opinion, if the law of war were included in the list of topics for codification.[15] It was *Mr. Sandström* (Sweden) — at last — who made the point that if the law of war belonged to the past, war itself still remained a reality. *Mr. Hsu* (China) followed this theme by stressing the possibility of a defensive war, which had to be envisaged, and expressed the opinion that it was essential to draw up regulations governing the law of war.[16] Deviating from the general rule of the ILC secretariat against expressing a definite opinion on questions submitted to the Commission, *Mr. Liang* (Secretary) felt obliged to state that the Commission should exclude the law of war from its subjects for codification, since the Charter had clearly condemned the previous conception that war was a natural calamity creating a situation in which the two parties concerned were on an equal footing and enjoyed equal rights.[17] Since the majority of the ILC was opposed to including the law of war on the list of topics for codification, the Chairman decided that the subject of neutrality should not be retained on the list either.[18]

The decision of the ILC represents a habit of mind, the consequences of which were particularly detrimental for the rules of naval warfare, since this part of the law of nations is mostly customary and not formally laid down in treaty instruments duly ratified and entered into force. Even in those cases where we have pertinent conventions still in force between a certain number of States, doubts have been raised in some quarters whether they have passed into desuetude. The Hague Conventions of 1907 relative to the Laying of Automatic Submarine

15 *Op. cit.*, 51—53.

16 *Op. cit.*, 51.

17 *Op. cit.*, 54.

18 *Op. cit.*, 53.

Contact Mines[19] and concerning Bombardment by Naval Forces in Time of War[20] may be mentioned as examples.[21] As a few members of the ILC pointed out, the attempt to outlaw the resort to force in international relations has neither resulted in the abolition of the use of force nor rendered useless the law of war, including the law of naval warfare. The more than one hundred major international armed conflicts since the founding of the United Nations bear ample witness to this fact.[22]

The tragic mistake of the ILC had another disadvantage. Due to its regrettable refusal it was left entirely to the International Committee of the Red Cross (ICRC) to take the initiative for the further development of the law of war. The ICRC has expertise and experience exclusively in the field of the so-called "Geneva" stream of the law of war, aimed at securing protection and humanitarian treatment for victims of international armed conflicts, namely the sick, wounded and shipwrecked, prisoners of war, and the civilian population in occupied territory.[23] To adapt the law of actual combat on the battlefield, let alone the law of naval warfare, to the rapidly changing political, economic, social and technological environment is quite a different task; it requires at a minimum a knowledge and understanding of the inherent difficulties of the so-called "Hague" stream of the law of war, dealing with the conduct of hostilities, including the use of methods and means of combat and the delimitation of targets.

As will be shown later, the ICRC and the CDDH have only reluctantly, or even inadvertently, modified some rules of naval warfare without facing up to the whole spectrum of existing problems. These efforts have centered around the basic problem of reviving the principle derived from the usages established among civilized peoples, from the laws of humanity and from the dictates of the public conscience within the meaning of the famous clause named after the Russian diplomat *Martens*,[24] that in all circumstances there must be a distinction made between combatants and non-combatants, military objectives and civilian objects.

---

[19] *Hinz/Rauch* (note 1), No. 1528; RGBl 1910, 231.

[20] *Hinz/Rauch* (note 1), No. 1529; RGBl 1910, 256.

[21] See, *R. R. Baxter*, Treaties and Custom, in: RdC vol. 129 (1970 I), 25—105 (97).

[22] As for the application of the law of naval warfare in international armed conflicts since 1945, see, *Rolf Ottmüller*, Die Anwendung von Seekriegsrecht in militärischen Konflikten seit 1945, Hamburg 1978.

[23] As for the distinction between Geneva and Hague law, see, *e.g.*, *Stanislaw E. Nahlik*, Droit dit de "Genève" et droit dit de "la Haye": Unicité ou dualité?, in: AFDI vol. 24 (1978), 9—17.

[24] See, the preamble of the Hague Convention No. IV Respecting the Laws and Customs of War on Land of 18 October 1907, in: *Hinz/Rauch* (note 1), No. 1503; RGBl 1910, 107; see also, Art. 1 par. 2 of Protocol I, in: *Hinz/Rauch* (note 1), No. 1570.

Immediately after World War II the ICRC resumed its endeavours to reform the two Geneva Conventions of 27 July 1929 for the Amelioration of the Conditions of the Wounded and Sick in Armed Forces in the Field and relative to the Treatment of Prisoners of War. The ICRC also continued work on the so-called "Tokyo draft", concerning the protection of the civilian population, which had been submitted to the XVth International Red Cross Conference in 1934.[25] These efforts resulted in a Diplomatic Conference, which ultimately adopted on 12 August 1949 the four Geneva Conventions, *i. e.* the Convention for the Amelioration of the Condition of the Wounded and Sick in Armed Forces in the Field (Convention I), the Convention for the Amelioration of the Condition of Wounded, Sick and Shipwrecked Members of Armed Forces at Sea (Convention II), the Convention relative to the Treatment of Prisoners of War (Convention III), and the Convention relative to the Protection of Civilian Persons in Time of War (Convention IV).[26]

The so-called "Hague"stream of the law of war remained basically unchanged, with little movement beyond the codifications achieved at the Hague Peace Conferences convened by Imperial Russia in 1899 and 1907.[27] Apart from some specific treaties *e. g.*, the Geneva Protocol of 17 June 1925 for the Prohibition of the Use in War of Asphyxiating, Poisonous or other Gases and of Bacteriological Methods of Warfare,[28] and the Convention of 10 April 1972 on the Prohibition of the Development, Production and Stockpiling of Bacteriological (Biological) and Toxic Weapons and on their Destruction,[29] this situation lasted until 1977. In that year the CDDH, which had been convened three years earlier by the Swiss Federal Council at the insistence of the ICRC, successfully concluded its work.

After four sessions in Geneva, two protocols were adopted. In contrast to the four Geneva Conventions of 1949 and despite its misleading heading, Protocol I regulates the conduct of hostilities and the pertinent treaty provisions apply to any land, air or sea warfare. It is no secret that it is precisely because of this extensive scope of coverage that no major military power has up until now ratified Protocol I.[30]

---

[25] See, *Anton Schlögel*, Geneva Red Cross Conventions and Protocols, in: *Rudolf Bernhardt* (ed.), Encyclopedia of Public International Law, Amsterdam 1982, vol. 3, 181—191 (183, 184).

[26] *Hinz/Rauch* (note 1), Nos. 1540, 1545, 1550, 1560; UNTS vol. 75 (1950), 31, 85, 135 and 287; BGBl 1954 II, 783, 813, 838, 917.

[27] Twelve of these Hague Conventions are reproduced in *Hinz/Rauch* (note 1), Nos. 1500—1504, 1526—1530, 1535 and 1537; RGBl 1910, 59—375.

[28] *Hinz/Rauch* (note 1), No. 1519; LNTS vol. 94 (1929), 65.

[29] *Hinz/Rauch* (note 1), No. 1521; BGBl 1983 II, 133.

[30] As for the States that have deposited their instrument of ratification, see, *Hinz/Rauch* (note 1), No. 1570 note 2.

The attempt to analyze the new rules of law applicable in armed conflict at sea cannot be discharged successfully without also taking into consideration a major development in another branch of international law, the law of the sea. The adoption of the new United Nations Convention on the Law of the Sea (LOS Convention)[31] on 10 December 1982 in Montego Bay, Jamaica, has justly been hailed as an epochal achievement. For the first time in history mankind has a written constitution for almost three quarters of the world's surface. To quote the former head of the United States delegation to the Third United Nations Conference on the Law of the Sea (UNCLOS III), Ambassador *Elliot Richardson:* "This is not a victory for any one country or any one ideology or any one point of view. It is a victory for the principle of peaceful cooperation and the rule of law."[32]

The League of Nations Conference for the Codification of International Law, held in 1936 in The Hague, had previously tried to lay down basic rules of the law of the sea, but to no avail. UNCLOS I succeeded in 1958 in adopting four Conventions, the Convention on the High Seas, the Convention on the Territorial Sea and the Contiguous Zone, the Convention on the Continental Shelf and the Convention on Fishing and Conservation of the Living Resources of the High Seas.[33] But one question of particular importance to the law of naval warfare had not been solved. All efforts to agree on the breadth of the territorial sea failed. Therefore the UN in 1960 convened UNCLOS II which was devoted exclusively to this issue. Again, no agreement on 3, 6 or 12 nautical miles could be reached.[34]

On 18 December 1972, the General Assembly of the UN requested the Secretary General to convene UNCLOS III, which would be charged with the establishment of an equitable international regime for the deep seabed and ocean floor beyond the limits of national jurisdiction and its resources, and with a broad range of traditional law of the sea issues, including those concerning the legal regimes of the high seas, the continental shelf, the territorial sea, international straits, fishing and conservation of living resources, the preservation of the marine environment and scientific research.[35] After eleven sessions and 9 years of arduous protracted negotiations, the Conference on 30 April 1982 adopt-

---

[31] UN Doc. A/CONF. 62/122 of 26 November 1982; the text of the Convention is reproduced in ILM vol. 21 (1982), 1261—1345.

[32] Wireless Bulletin from Washington, 2 September 1980.

[33] UNTS vol. 450 (1963), 82; vol. 516 (1964), 206; vol. 499 (1964), 312; vol. 559 (1966), 285.

[34] See, *Günther Hoog,* Die Genfer Seerechtskonferenzen von 1958 und 1960, Frankfurt a. M./Berlin 1961, 15, 30.

[35] GA Resolution 3029 (XXVII) of 24 January 1973.

ed the new LOS Convention by a record-breaking vote, taken at the request of the delegation of the United States. The result was 130 in favour, 4 against, with 17 abstentions. The four votes against the adoption of the Convention were cast by the United States, Venezuela, Turkey and Israel.[36] The Final Act of UNCLOS III[37] was signed in Montego Bay on 10 December 1982 by 140 participating States and 9 other entities.[38] The same day the Convention was opened for signature. 117 States and two other entities[39] became signatories.[40] The LOS Convention will enter into force 12 months after the date of deposit of the sixtieth instrument of ratification or accession.[41] It should be mentioned in this context that the new LOS Convention will not replace the four 1958 Conventions on the Law of the Sea; it will simply prevail over the earlier treaties where inconsistencies exist.[42]

There has never been any doubt that UNCLOS III was dealing exclusively with the law of peace and that it did not intend to touch upon the law of naval warfare. Nonetheless, there are ramifications in the new LOS Convention which affect the conduct of belligerent operations at sea. The legitimate breadth of the territorial sea of a neutral State, for instance, and the legal situation in straits or archipelagic sea lanes bordered by neutral states, are of tremendous importance for the naval forces in times of war.

As will be shown, there are also areas of the law of naval warfare which will be influenced twice over, both by the work of the CDDH and of UNCLOS III.

---

[36] For details, see, *Elmar Rauch*, Die Sowjetunion und die Entwicklung des Seevölkerrechts, Berlin 1982, 361 *et seq.*

[37] UN Doc. A/CONF. 62/121 of 21 October 1982, reproduced in ILM vol. 21 (1982), 1245—1260.

[38] The signatories of the Final Act appear in ILM vol. 21 (1982), 1477.

[39] The two entities are the UN Councils on Namibia and the Cook Islands.

[40] The complete list of signatories of the Convention appears in ILM vol. 21 (1982), 1477.

[41] Art. 308 par. 1.

[42] Art. 311 par. 1.

II. Armed Conflict at Sea in general

Traditionally there have to be distinguished two main areas of the law of naval warfare: (i) the rules applied in the context of belligerent action against the enemy's fleet or against military objectives on land, and (ii) the rules governing naval measures against the maritime commerce of the enemy (the law of prize). This chapter shall focus on some issues of a general character.

1. National Liberation Movements and Warships

By definition war is an armed conflict between subjects of international law. Until 1977 only States were recognized as subjects of the law of war within this meaning. Although the UN General Assembly had repeatedly confirmed the right of liberation movements to have recourse to all necessary means of resistance, including a *ius ad bellum,* and to invoke the *ius in bello,*[43] these resolutions did not change the law. They could be considered only as starting points for the possible development of customary international law.

Protocol I became the breakthrough for this new concept. As for its scope of application, Art. 1 par. 3 includes situations referred to in Art. 2 common to the Geneva Conventions of 12 August 1949, *i. e.,* to all cases of declared war or of any other armed conflict "between States". In addition, par. 4 of Art. 1 extends the applicability of Protocol I to armed conflicts in which peoples in the exercise of their right of self-determination are fighting against colonial domination, alien occupation, or racist regimes. In other words, certain types of internal conflicts within a State are assimilated to conflicts of an international character. Art. 96 par. 3 of Protocol I provides that the authority representing a people engaged against a State in an armed conflict of this type may unilaterally declare the willingness to submit to the law of war as contained in the Geneva Conventions and Protocol I. Such declaration shall, upon its receipt by the depositary, have the effect that the Conventions and the Protocol are brought into force for the said authority as a party to the conflict and that the treaties mentioned are equally binding upon all parties to the conflict. This important change is the basis for the ap-

[43] GA Resolution 2621 (XXV) of 21 October 1970 and GA Resolution 3103 (XXVIII) of 8 January 1974.

plication of Art. 43 and 44 of Protocol I, dealing with armed forces, combatants and prisoners of war.

The armed forces of national liberation movements according to Art. 43 consist of all organized armed forces, groups and units which are under a command responsible to the party for the conduct of its subordinates. Such armed forces must be subject to an internal disciplinary system which, *inter alia,* shall enforce compliance with the rules of the law of war. Art. 44 par. 3 provides that the guerilla fighter who cannot distinguish himself from the civilian population shall retain his status as a combatant provided he meets certain minimum requirements, thus making an important exception to the traditional rules of the law of war. Even such guerillas, however, remain subject to the necessity of an internal disciplinary system.

The law of the sea and the law of naval warfare did not follow this negative precedent of reduced requirements of distinguishability as set by the CDDH. The definition of the term "warship" bears witness to that fact. The Second Hague Peace Conference of 1907, which drew up many conventions on the law of naval warfare, did not specifically agree on a definition of the term warship. However, the Hague Convention No. VII concerning the Conversion of Merchant Ships into Warships,[44] by enumerating the conditions that must be met in order to convert a merchant vessel into a warship, indirectly defined the latter. UNCLOS I in 1958 was the first to give a special legal definition for the term "warship" in the Convention on the High Seas.[45] This definition has been reaffirmed in Art. 29 of the 1982 LOS Convention. For the purpose of this new Convention, "warship" means a ship belonging to the armed forces of a State bearing the external marks distinguishing such ship's nationality, under the command of an officer duly commissioned by the government of the State and whose name appears in the appropriate service list or its equivalent, and manned by a crew which is under regular armed forces discipline.[46]

A threshold question here might be whether guerilla forces of a national liberation movement, who are subject to an internal disciplinary system within the meaning of Art. 43 of Protocol I, are under "regular" armed forces discipline within the sense of Art. 29 of the new LOS Convention. The exact delineation of the various categories of protected persons is one of the weakest points of the four Geneva Conventions of 1949 and of Protocol I. Lawful belligerents with a privileged

---

[44] *Hinz/Rauch* (note 1), No. 1527; RGBl 1910, 207.

[45] Art. 8 par. 2.

[46] Art. 29.

status on the one hand, and unlawful belligerents with an unprivileged status on the other, do not necessarily correspond to the distinction between regular combatants and irregular combatants.

Already under the Hague Regulations Respecting the Laws and Customs of War on Land (HR),[47] those inhabitants of a territory who, on the approach of the enemy, spontaneously take up arms to resist the invading troops without having had time to organize themselves, are entitled to be regarded as belligerents, if they carry arms openly and if they respect the laws and customs of war.[48] The members of such a *levée en masse* are lawful belligerents, but at the same time irregular combatants.[49] The first three Geneva Conventions of 1949 correctly add to the definition of the *levée en masse* the words "without having had time to organize themselves into 'regular' armed units".[50] These Conventions stipulate further that even members of regular armed forces who profess allegiance to a government or an authority not recognized by the detaining power, shall enjoy the protection afforded to lawful belligerents.[51] Since not only a government of a State is mentioned here, but also an "authority", it seems clear that national liberation movements may qualify as having "regular armed forces", *i. e.*, units with regular armed forces discipline within the meaning of Art. 29 of the new LOS Convention. It is therefore only a question of fact, to be decided on a case by case basis, whether armed forces of a liberation movement, including guerilla units, are actually under a regular or an irregular discipline, it being understood that even an irregular discipline suffices for Art. 43 and 44 of Protocol I.[52]

Even with this threshold question answered in the affirmative, however, Art. 29 of the LOS Convention makes a further requirement that a warship should belong to the armed forces[53] of a State. Since no

---

[47] *Hinz/Rauch* (note 1), No. 1504; RGBl 1910, 132.

[48] Art. 2 Hague Rules.

[49] See, *Richard R. Baxter*, So-called "Unprivileged Belligerency": Spies, Guerillas and Saboteurs, in: BYIL vol. 28 (1951), 323—344; *Herbert Schwab*, Irreguläre Kombattanten als Kriegsgefangene, Würzburg 1976.

[50] Art. 13 par. 6 Convention I; Art. 13 par. 6 Convention II; Art. 4 A par. 6 Convention III.

[51] Art. 13 par. 3 Convention I; Art. 13 par. 3 Convention II; Art. 4 A par. 3 Convention III.

[52] As to the interpretation of Art. 4 Convention III, see in particular, *Jean S. Picted* (ed.), The Geneva Conventions of 12 August 1949 (Commentary), vol. 3: *Jean de Preux*, III Geneva Convention, translated into English by *A. P. de Heney*, Geneva 1960, 61—64; according to this commentary it is a minimum requirement that the government or authority must be recognized by third States, although this is not expressly stated in the Convention. This consideration is allegedly consistent with the spirit of the provision which was founded on the specific case of the French forces of *General de Gaulle* in World War II (*op. cit.*, 63).

mention is made of an "authority" or other non-State entity, it follows that national liberation movement vessels are precluded from having "warship" status.

In armed conflict at sea only warships may exercise belligerent rights.[54] Thus the question arises as to the legal status of military ships of national liberation movements and in particular whether they are relegated to being pirate ships. As far as piracy is concerned, the new LOS Convention primarily repeats the provisions of the 1958 Convention on the High Seas.[55] "Piracy" under both these Conventions consists of any illegal acts of violence or detention, or any act of depredation, committed for private ends by the crew or the passengers of a private ship or a private aircraft and directed against another ship or aircraft, or against persons or property on board such ship or aircraft.[56] The acts of piracy, as defined, committed by a warship, government ship or government aircraft whose crew has mutinied and taken control of the ship or aircraft, are assimilated to acts committed by a private ship or aircraft.[57] The most important criterion in this context is that the acts have to be committed for "private ends". The fight of peoples against colonial domination, alien occupation, or racist regimes, in the exercise of the right of self-determination, is never, however, an undertaking for private ends. Ships used for military purposes by national liberation movements thus cannot, in my opinion, be regarded as pirate ships. The Soviet Manual of Naval Warfare comes to the opposite conclusion.[58]

Under the law of the sea these ships should, it seems to me, be assimilated to government ships operated for non-commercial purposes.[59] Such an analogy is supported by the mandatory dispute settlement system in the new LOS Convention, which contains an optional clause whereby a party may exclude from its scope "military activities", including military activities by government vessels and aircraft engaged in non-commercial service.[60]

---

[53] Art. 8 par. 2 of the High Seas Convention of 1958 uses the language "belonging to the naval forces of a State".

[54] US Office of Naval Operations, Law of Naval Warfare, Washington 1955 (in the following abbreviated "US LNW"), NWIP 10—2, No. 500 e, and Ministry of Defense of the USSR, Voenno-morskoj meždunarodno-pravovoj spravočnik (Naval International Law Manual), Moscow 1966 (in the following abbreviated "USSR NILM"), 433—434.

[55] See, Arts. 14—22 of the High Seas Convention.

[56] Art. 101.

[57] Art. 102.

[58] USSR NILM (note 54), 433.

[59] See, Arts. 31, 32, 96, 102, 236.

[60] Art. 298 par. 1 (b).

Whatever the difficulty involved in determining the precise status of military ships of national liberation movements under the law of the sea, even an assimilation to government vessels in time of peace cannot make such quasi-public vessels a man-of-war. There exists a gap between the development of the law of armed conflict and of the law of the sea which cannot be bridged by way of interpretation or analogy. National liberation movements cannot have "warships".

2. Perfidy and Ruses of War

The condemnation of perfidy is derived from the principle of chivalry and is an uncontested ancient precept of the laws and customs of war. Protocol I contributes to clarify the meaning of the terms perfidy and ruses of war by giving specific definitions and by spelling out detailed provisions on this subject. Perfidy constitutes acts inviting the confidence of an adversary to lead him to believe that he is entitled to, or is obliged to accord, protection under the rules of international law applicable in armed conflict, with the intent of betraying that confidence.[61] Stratagems or ruses of war, on the other hand, are acts which are intended to mislead an adversary or to induce him to act recklessly, but which infringe upon no rule of international law applicable in armed conflict and which are not perfidious because they do not invite the confidence of an adversary with respect to protection under that law.[62] The uses of camouflage, decoys, mock operations, feigned attacks, dummy ships, or misinformation are well known examples of such ruses.[63]

The ruse which is of the most practical importance in naval warfare is the use of the false flag. Both the new LOS Convention and Protocol I reaffirm and develop the law concerning the use of flags. According to Art. 91 of the LOS Convention, every State shall fix the conditions for the grant of its nationality to ships, for the registration of ships in its territory, and for the right to fly its flag. Ships have the nationality of the State whose flag they are entitled to fly, subject to the over-reaching requirement that a genuine link exists between that State and the ship. Art. 92 of the new LOS Convention provides that ships shall sail under the flag of one State only and shall be subject to its exclusive jurisdiction on the high seas. A ship may not change its flag during a voyage or while in a port of call save in the case of a real transfer of ownership or change of registry. These rules were already

[61] Art. 37 par. 1.

[62] Art. 37 par. 2.

[63] Art. 37 par. 2, last sentence.

contained in the 1958 High Seas Convention.[64] There is, however, in the 1982 LOS Convention a new article on the question of ships flying the flag of the United Nations, its specialized agencies, and the International Atomic Energy Agency. This is important, even if the provision is limited by the declaration that the new LOS Convention does not prejudice the question of ships flying the flag of these organizations.[65]

These rules are part of the law of peace. As for naval warfare, custom allows for a belligerent warship to use false colors and to disguise her outward appearance in other ways in order to deceive the enemy, provided that prior to going into action, such warship shows her true colors.[66] The celebrated German cruiser *Emden* and *Count Luckner's 'Seeadler'* were extremely successful in using this stratagem during World War I.[67]

There seems to be some dispute whether a merchant vessel is entitled to deceive enemy warships in the same way. While there is no multilateral convention that regulates this question, some national laws and ordinances are quite specific. The British Merchant Shipping Act of 1894, *e. g.*, provides that if a person uses the British flag for the purpose of making a non-British ship appear to be a British one, the ship shall be subject to forfeiture, unless such ruse is effected for the purpose of escaping capture by an enemy or by a foreign ship of war in the exercise of some belligerent right.[68] The US Neutrality Act of 1939, in contrast, made it unlawful for any vessel belonging to or operating under the jurisdiction of any foreign State to use the flag of the United States thereon, or to make use of any distinctive signs or markings, indicating that the same is an American vessel.[69] During World War II the practice of false flags on merchant vessels gave rise to quite a number of diplomatic protests, including by Denmark, the Netherlands and Japan.[70]

---

[64] Arts. 5 and 6.

[65] Art. 93.

[66] See, the Manuals of the Law of Naval Warfare, *e. g.*, US LNW (note 54) NWIP 10—2, No. 640 a and note 54 for Chapter 6; USSR NILM (note 54), 457, 458. The German Prize Ordinance of 28 August 1939 (RGBl 1939 I, 1585) provides in Art. 57: "Das anzuhaltende Fahrzeug wird durch Signal oder durch einen Warnschuß zum Stoppen aufgefordert. Spätestens mit dieser Aufforderung setzt das Kriegsschiff seine Flagge." The German Prize Ordinance of 1909/1914 (RGBl 1914, 275) stipulated in No. 82: "Während der Jagd ist ein Zeigen der Kriegsflagge nicht erforderlich, die Führung jeder beliebigen Handelsflagge statthaft ..."

[67] Note 42 for Chapter 6; see also, *H. A. Smith*, The Law and Custom of the Sea, 2nd ed., London 1950, 91.

[68] Section 69 par. 1.

[69] Section 14 a.

[70] Urkunden zum Seekriegsrecht, zusammengestellt vom Oberkommando der Kriegsmarine, 1. Abt. Seekriegsleitung, Berlin 1941, Nos. 151—155.

In the past various attempts have been made to eliminate this discrepancy between the law of the sea and the law of naval warfare. The Manual of the Laws of Naval War governing the Relations between Belligerents, adopted in 1913 by the Institut de Droit International, treated the use of false flags as *"moyen perfide et barbarois"*.[71] Likewise, the Draft Law of Naval War, adopted by the International Law Association in 1920, prohibited the use of false flags as being treacherous and barbaric.[72] Further, in the 1967 Draft Manual of the Law of Naval Warfare of the Federal Republic of Germany, the question was asked whether, with respect to the use of false colors, the difference between land-warfare and air-warfare on the one hand and naval warfare on the other could continue to be maintained and justified, since false colors contribute to a basic blurring of the distinction between combatants and civilians.[73]

It is an important clarification, therefore, that in the context of the rules regarding prohibition of perfidy and the protection of recognized emblems and emblems of nationality, the CDDH by way of exception adopted a stipulation that nothing in Protocol I shall affect the existing generally recognized rules of international law applicable to the use of flags in the conduct of armed conflict at sea.[74] It is true that this is only a reference to the existing body of law and not an express declaration that the use of false colors in naval war is indeed a legitimate stratagem. In view of the intensive work of the CDDH on Section I of Part III of Protocol I, however, this language as a practical matter virtually amounts to a recognition of the centuries old practice.

At the same time, Protocol I raises a new and interesting problem: whether the traditional rule applies to the use of the flag of the United Nations and its specialized agencies or other international organizations, *e. g.*, the future International Seabed Authority.[75] As an example of perfidy, Art. 37 par. 1 (d) of Protocol I mentions the feigning of protected status by the use of "signs, emblems or uniforms of the United Nations or of neutral or other States not parties to the conflict." The term "emblem" includes flags as evidenced by Art. 38[76] and Art. 39.[77] The

---

[71] *Marcel Deltentre*, Recueil général de Lois et Coutumes de la Guerre, Bruxelles 1943, 666 *et seq.*

[72] International Law Association, Report of the 29th Conference, 27—31 May 1920, London 1920, 169 *et seq.*

[73] Zentrale Dienstvorschrift (ZDv) 15/12 (draft), Kriegsvölkerrecht, Leitfaden für den Unterricht (Teil 9) — Seekriegsrecht — (Lehrschrift), Bonn 1967, 32.

[74] Art. 39 par. 3.

[75] See, Arts. 156—185 and Annex IV LOS Convention, Arts. 91, 92 LOS Convention, and Arts. 38, 39 Protocol I.

[76] Art. 38 includes in par. 1 the flag of truce as an recognized emblem.

flag of the World Organisation, therefore, seems to be assimilated to those of neutral States and the exception in Art. 39, mentioned above, expressly includes Art. 37 par. 1 (d).

At first glance, the UN flag might seem to be a new legitimate disguise for belligerent warships. In this context, however, it must not be overlooked that Protocol I makes a fine distinction between emblems of nationality[78] and recognized emblems.[79] The emblem of the United Nations is dealt with in the context of recognized emblems. In other words, there is an analogy between the UN flag and the Red Cross flag. From the protection of recognized emblems in Art. 36 there is no exception provided for in Art. 39 par. 3, whose scope of application extends exclusively to Art. 37 par. 1 (d) and Art. 39 itself. It is misleading and a case of bad drafting indeed that the UN flag is even mentioned in Art. 37 par. 1 (d); a stipulation from which Art. 39 par. 3 provides for an exception on behalf of naval warfare, while an unrestricted protection of the UN flag is contained in Art. 38. It is my point of view that the use of the UN flag by belligerent warship would be an act of perfidy and not a legitimate ruse of war.

3. Normal Mode of Navigation for Submarines

The LOS Convention of 1982 has contributed to clearing up to some extent the controversy and uncertainty which have marked the interpretation and application of the principle that belligerents are forbidden to use neutral ports and waters as a base of naval operations against their adversaries. The problem in question is the extent to which a neutral may permit repairs of submarines while in its port.

In accordance with the Hague Convention No. XIII of 18 October 1907 concerning the Rights and Duties of Neutral Powers in Naval War, belligerent warship in neutral ports and roadsteads may only carry out such repairs as are absolutely necessary to render them "seaworthy", and may not add in any manner whatsoever to their fighting force. The local authorities of the neutral Power shall decide what

[77] Art. 39 is under the heading "Emblems of nationality"; par. 1 and 2 read as follows:

"(1) It is prohibited to make use in an armed conflict of the flags or military emblems, insignia or uniforms of neutral or other States not Parties to the Conflict.

(2) It is prohibited to make use of the flags or military emblems, insignia or uniforms of adverse Parties while engaging in attacks or in order to shield, favour, protect or impede military operations."

[78] Art. 39.

[79] Art. 38.

repairs are necessary, and these must be carried out with the least possible delay.[80] This rule has been interpreted in contradicting ways. Leaving aside the unsettled question whether a neutral's duty includes forbidding under any circumstances the repair of damage incurred in battle,[81] the issue that has been brought closer to a solution by UNCLOS III is the dispute as to whether a submarine is seaworthy if it is able to navigate only on the surface.

In 1944 the German submarine U-760 suffered severe damage by air attacks near the Azore Islands and later suffered additional damage by depth charges in the Bay of Biscay. Unable to submerge, it took refuge in the port of Vigo in neutral Spain. The United States in this incident took the position that a submarine's seaworthiness does not include the capability of submerged navigation.[82] In my opinion this decision was wrong at the time and still is. In particular, modern submarines are designed and built to navigate and to operate primarily in the submerged mode. This is vividly illustrated by the fact that they can travel faster submerged than on the surface. They are also far easier to handle and safe to maneuver in confined areas and congested waters in a submerged position. It is almost impossible to make a clear-cut distinction between a seaworthy and a battleworthy warship. In a great number of cases, to make a vessel seaworthy is, in effect, to make her battleworthy, and in a strict sense any repairs, irrespective of the cause of the damage, in restoring seaworthiness will necessarily have an effect on battleworthiness.

The Hague Convention No. XIII addresses only "warships" without any distinction between surface and subsurface vessels. Submarines, although known, were not treated separately, and airplanes were left out entirely. The term "seaworthiness" appears in Articles 17 and 21 of Hague XIII. The provision on repairs in neutral ports was based upon a British proposal which read: "A neutral State must not knowingly permit a warship of a belligerent to make repairs in excess of what will be necessary for navigating."[83] The term "necessary for navigating"

[80] Arts. 5 and 17 of the Hague Convention XIII; see, *Hinz/Rauch* (note 1), No. 1537.

[81] The Hague Convention XIII, however, makes no distinction between damage produced by enemy fire and damage produced by the sea. And a warship does not necessarily add to his fighting force any more by repairing damage incurred in battle than by repairing damage caused by the sea. Thus Hague XIII would appear to allow either interpretation; see, US LNW (note 54) NWIP 10—2, note 33 for Chapter 4.

[82] ZDv 15/12 draft (note 73), 209.

[83] *James Brown Scott,* The Proceedings of the Hague Peace Conferences. The Conference of 1907, Oxford 1920, vol. III, 694, Annex 44; Art. 19 of the Convention.

reappears in the Committee Report.[84] The Japanese delegation submitted a proposal which used the language: "Belligerent ships cannot in neutral ports or waters increase their war forces nor make repairs other than those indispensable to their safety in sailing."[85] The President of the Committee explained this suggestion to mean the permissibility of repairs "indispensable to safe navigation under all circumstances".[86] The Russian representative also stressed that his delegation believed that whatever the cause of the damage to a warship, the authorities of a neutral port may permit a warship to make all repairs that are "indispensable to safe navigation".[87]

The new LOS Convention provides some authoritative guidance on this subject in the context of the transit passage regime through straits[88] and the archipelagic sea lanes passage regime.[89] Both regimes are defined to include the exercise of the freedom of navigation "in the normal mode"[90] solely for the purpose of continuous, expeditious and unobstructed transit between one part of the high seas or an exclusive economic zone and another part of the high seas or an exclusive economic zone. There was no need to insert the term "normal mode" here, because the right or freedom of navigation as such includes the right to submerged passage. This has been so since the appearance of the submarine and under the 1958 Convention on the High Seas, the term of art "freedom of navigation" included the submerged passage of submarines.[91] If submarines are for some reason required to navigate on the surface, this would be an exception restricting the normal right of navigation. Such

---

[84] *Scott* (note 83), vol. I, 308.

[85] Art. 4; see, *Scott* (note 83) vol. III, 702.

[86] *Scott* (note 83) vol. III, 606.

[87] *Op. cit.*, 608.

[88] Arts. 34—44.

[89] Art. 53.

[90] Art. 53 par. 3; Art. 39 par. 1 (c).

[91] *E. g.* Art. 2. It would transgress the scope of this paper to repeat the discussion on the interpretation of the strait chapter of the LOS Convention. I may restrict myself to a reference to my analysis, in: *Elmar Rauch*, Die Sowjetunion und die Entwicklung des Seevölkerrechts, Berlin 1982, 77—89, 140, 250, 288—295, and the literature quoted there, in particular *W. Michael Reismann*, The Regime of Straits and National Security: An Appraisal of International Lawmaking, in: AJIL vol. 74 (1980), 48—76, and *John Norton Moore*, The Regime of Straits and the Third United Nations Conference on the Law of the Sea, in: *op. cit.*, 77—121. Those who critizise that the Convention does not contain an express reference to submerged passage do not pay attention to the problem of negative implication. If the Part on straits and transit passage included such an unnecessary clarification it might be argued that the term navigation used in the regime for the exclusive economic zone would exclude submerged passage. If the word "normal" carries any meaning at all, good faith interpretation in accordance with Art. 31 par. 1 of the Law of Treaties has to construe it as including subsurface navigation for sub-marines.

a restriction would have to be expressly stated, as in the case of the right of innocent passage.[92] Although unnecessary, the insertion of the term "normal mode" makes it even more graphic that no restriction can ever be implied that would detract from the general right of submarines to navigate submerged.

A submarine is seaworthy if it is capable of navigating in the normal mode. This "normal mode" concept of the new LOS Convention should help put to rest once and for all the problem of interpretation concerning Hague XIII of 1907 with respect to the repair of submarines. Even more so since the law of neutrality is part of the international law of peace, modified by the state of war between two other subjects of international law, rather than a part of the law of war.[93]

[92] See, Art. 14 par. 6 of the 1958 Convention on the Territorial Sea and the Contiguous Zone; Art. 20 LOS Convention.

[93] *Friedrich Berber*, Lehrbuch des Völkerrechts, vol. II: Kriegsrecht, München/Berlin 1962, 215.

III. Area of Naval Operations

The general area within which naval forces have traditionally been permitted to conduct operations includes the high seas, the territorial sea and internal waters of the belligerents, the land territory accessible to naval forces and the superjacent airspace over such waters and territory. At a time when the seas were classified under three headings only — internal waters, territorial sea, and high seas — there were no significant difficulties. Under the new LOS Convention, however, we now have to deal with archipelagic waters, exclusive economic zones, and an international area beyond the limits of national jurisdiction on the seabed and ocean floor, as well as with a special regime for international straits and archipelagic sea lanes. These new concepts to some degree put the adequacy of the traditional rules of war and neutrality at sea in question. This chapter will try to identify some of the more important ramifications of UNCLOS III upon the activities of belligerents and neutrals in times of armed conflict.

1. Territorial Sea

The LOS Convention reaffirms the customary international law as already codified in the 1958 Convention on the Territorial Sea and the Contiguous Zone. Art. 2 of the LOS Convention provides that the sovereignty of a coastal State extends beyond its land territory and internal waters to an adjacent belt of sea, described as the territorial sea. Functionally the territorial sea remains, therefore, unchanged.[94]

The new development consists in the Convention codifying the trend away from the 3 nautical mile territorial sea in favour of a maximum of 12 nautical miles. This should be the end of a hotly disputed issue which has continued to fester since UNCLOS II failed in 1960 to establish with more certainty the maximum breadth of the territorial waters of a coastal State.[95] State practice has been widely divergent on this issue. A great number of newly independent countries in particular have declared territorial seas between 12 and 200 nautical miles. In current State practice, as of 1 May 1983, 87 coastal States already claim a 12

[94] See, Art. 1 and 2 of the 1958 Convention on the Territorrial Sea and the Contiguous Zone.

[95] See, *supra*, 9.

miles territorial sea, 15 States consider a 200 nautical miles wide belt of water their territorial sea, only 18 are content with the traditional breadth of 3 nautical miles, 10 States claim a territorial sea between 15 and 150 nautical miles, and 7 coastal States have a territorial sea between 4 and 6 nautical miles.[96]

As a matter of principle belligerents are bound to respect the sovereignty of neutral powers and to abstain, in neutral territory or neutral waters, from any act of warfare. Any act of hostility, including capture and the exercise of the right of search, committed by belligerent warships in the territorial waters of a neutral power, constitutes a violation of neutrality and is strictly forbidden.[97]

2. Archipelagic Waters

The concept of sovereignty over a belt of water off the coast has been extended by UNCLOS III for archipelagic States by creating for the first time in a multilateral Convention the term "archipelagic waters". It should be stressed that this new concept applies only to archipelagic States, *i. e.* insular States constituted wholly by one or more archipelagos, and not to mainland States who possess island groupings.[98] In this way UNCLOS III channelled and restricted an emerging State practice of using archipelagic principles as a pretext for extending coastal State sovereignty over large areas of the high seas. The archipelagic State may draw straight archipelagic baselines joining the outermost points of the outermost islands and drying reefs of its archipelago, subject to certain conditions prescribed in detail in the Convention.[99] The territorial sea, the contiguous zone, the exclusive economic zone and the continental shelf are measured from these baselines.[100]

As to the legal status of general archipelagic waters, of the air space over those waters, and of their bed and subsoil, there is no difference from the traditional concept of the territorial sea. That means that the sovereignty of an archipelagic State extends to the waters enclosed by the above mentioned baselines, regardless of their depth or distance from the coast, to the superjacent airspace and the underlying sea bed and subsoil.[101]

---

[96] Nachrichten für Seefahrer, Heft 20/1983, Beilage "Ansprüche der Staaten auf Meereszonen", issued by the Federal Ministry of Transportation.

[97] Art. 1 Hague Convention XIII; US LNW (note 54), No. 440; USSR NILM (note 54), 472, 473.

[98] Art. 46.

[99] Art. 47.

[100] Art. 48.

[101] Art. 49.

As neutrality as a legal concept is nothing else but a natural attribute of the right of sovereignty of States not parties to the conflict, the belligerents in future will have to respect archipelagic waters the same way as they have to respect the territorial sea of the coastal State. They will have to abstain in archipelagic waters of neutral States from any act of warfare, including capture and the exercise of the right of search. By way of analogy, all rules contained in Hague XIII concerning the territorial sea of neutral powers will have to be applied *mutatis mutandis* to archipelagic waters of neutral archipelagic States. The ramifications of limited enforcement capacity of certain developing archipelagic States in their huge expanses of water on this balance will be dealt with in sub-chapter seven *infra*.

3. Exclusive Economic Zone

In contrast to archipelagic waters, the new concept of the exclusive economic zone creates difficulties. It is a 200 nautical mile wide belt of water (measured from the baseline from which the territorial sea is measured) beyond and adjacent to the territorial sea, subject to the specific legal regime established in Part V of the new LOS Convention.[102] We are faced with a legal status *sui generis*, neither sovereignty of the coastal State,[103] nor high seas status.[104] In terms of space as well as of law, the exclusive economic zone lies between both of them. It is the synthesis of the fisheries zone, epicontinental sea, patrimonial sea, and continental shelf concept which started with the Truman Proclamation of 1945.[105] The coastal State has certain specific sovereign rights, jurisdiction and other rights.[106] These terms of art mean coastal State jurisdiction of a different intensity than full sovereignty.[107] In addition to jurisdiction over all living and non-living resources within the 200 nautical mile exclusive economic zone, the new LOS Convention permits the exercise of coastal State jurisdiction over marine scientific research, protection and preservation of the marine environment, the establishment and use of artificial islands, and the establishment and use of installations and structures with economic purposes. The LOS Convention, however, explicitly preserves for all States the high sea freedoms of navigation and overflight and all other internationally lawful

[102] Arts. 55 and 57.

[103] Compare Art. 2, Art. 49 (sovereignty).

[104] Arts. 86, 87, 89 (freedom for all States).

[105] See, *Rauch* (note 91), 91—100.

[106] See, Art. 56.

[107] For a more detailed discussion of the difference between sovereignty and jurisdiction and the various types of jurisdiction, see, *Rauch* (note 91), 94, 95.

uses of the sea not falling within coastal State jurisdiction.[108] Consequently, all customary military uses of the high seas, including maneuvers, weapons exercises, gunnery training etc., are lawful in the exclusive economic zone of third States.[109]

It was Sweden, a traditionally neutral country, that during the UNCLOS III process consistently addressed the problem of the relationship between the new LOS Convention and the law of naval warfare. Already in 1974 the official journal of the Swedish Navy published an anonymous article dealing with the problem of the exclusive economic zone of a neutral State. This treatise reads in part: "For Sweden it is of great interest to prevent, that other States use our exclusive economic zone for the deployment of nuclear weapons. The coastal State has to make sure that this does not happen ... In times of war the neutral State has the obligation under the 1907 Convention to protect its merchant navy and those of other States against military operations. The neutral State is also obliged to prevent the use of its sea territory by a belligerent as a base for naval operations against the adverse party. The rights and duties layed upon the coastal States in the exclusive economic zone will also have to be fulfilled in situations where the coastal State remains neutral in a war between third powers. The protection of neutrality in this case is evidently — in whole or in part — extended to the exclusive economic zone."[110]

The position taken in the treatise is thus based upon a rather vague reference to a coastal State's "sea territory", and it proceeds on assumptions that do not stand up to legal analysis. The statements and declarations made by the Swedish delegation at UNCLOS III were even more ambiguous. Time and again the Swedish representative made obscure references to the Hague Conventions of 1907. It may suffice to quote just the last three pertinent statements. On 26 August 1980, during the Ninth Session, the Swedish representative referred to the question of the relationship between the new Convention on the Law of the Sea and the Conventions relating to the laws of war and the law of neutrality, the latter being a field to which Sweden attached great importance. The question was also linked to the wider problem of how the Convention on the Law of the Sea was to operate in times of war for both belligerent and neutral States. It was his delegation's understanding that the rights and obligations resulting from the conventions on the laws of warfare and on neutrality, particularly the Hague Conventions of 1907, would not be affected by the new law of the sea.[111]

---

[108] Art. 58.

[109] See, *Rauch* (note 91), 96—100, 140—148.

[110] Några aktuella havsrättsfrågor, in: Sveriges Flotta vol. 70 (1974), 8—11.

During the Eleventh Session, on 31 March 1982, the Swedish delegate made basically the same statement in plenary.[112] At the final session of UNCLOS III in Montego Bay, Jamaica, the head of the Swedish delegation stated: "The Convention contains in Article 311 an important provision regarding the relation to other conventions and international agreements. We are not convinced that this Article will in practice solve all problems that may arise in this connection. Since Sweden pursues a policy aiming at neutrality in times of war, we have given special attention to the relationship between the Convention and the rules of neutrality in case of war. It is our understanding that the Convention does not affect the rights and duties of a neutral State provided for in the Convention of 18 October 1907 concerning the Rights and Duties of Neutral Powers in Case of Naval Warfare."[113] Again, this is a rather obscure statement, since our problem does not relate to any change in the Hague Conventions of 1907 due to the new LOS Convention, but concerns the issue of whether, or to what extent, the new concept of the exclusive economic zone comes within the scope of the Conventions of the Hague Peace Conference of 1907 as far as the law of naval warfare is concerned.

One may even see a certain contradiction in the following remarks by the Swedish ambassador to UNCLOS III made at the same Jamaica plenary session: "There are also other aspects of the law of the sea which are not dealt with in the Convention but which are worthy of our attention. For instance, the rules of armed conflict at sea are clearly in need of revision. Indeed some work still remains to be done before we have a complete and coherent system of international law relating to all uses of the sea."[114]

At any rate, these statements at the conference are not very helpful. In order to analyze the problem, one may look to the authenticated French version of the new LOS Convention,[115] since the 1907 Hague Convention No. XIII is authentic only in French. It is true that the LOS Convention uses the terms *droit souverain* and *juridiction* to describe the competences of the coastal State in the exclusive economic zone, and that precisely the same terms are used in the 1907 Hague Convention No. XIII.[116] This does not mean, however, that the new concept of the exclusive economic zone is *nunc pro tunc* to be included

[111] UN Doc. A/CONF. 62/SR. 136 of 26 August 1980, 16.

[112] UN Doc. A/CONF. 62/SR. 163 of 6 April 1982, 3.

[113] UN Doc. A/CONF. 62/PV 187 of 26 January 1983, 97.

[114] *Ibid.*

[115] Art. 320.

[116] Arts. 1, 3 and 8.

in the historical scope of application of the Convention regarding the Rights and Duties of Neutral Powers in Naval War. A treaty has to be interpreted in accordance with the ordinary meaning to be given to the terms of the treaty in their full context and in the light of the specific treaty's object and purpose.[117]

In 1907 diplomats, lawyers, and naval officers knew only of the high seas and the territorial waters of coastal States. There was no dispute whatsoever that all jurisdictional zones which went beyond the territorial sea, *i. e.*, fisheries zones, security zones, customs zones, sanitary zones an other "contiguous" zones, remained constituent parts of the high seas in times of peace as well as in times of war. Concepts or ideas of an economic zone with a legal status *sui generis* were undreamed of at that time. This was true even 35 years later, when in 1958 UNCLOS I adopted the Convention on the Territorial Sea and the Contiguous Zone. The latter zone had nothing in common with the concept of sovereignty of the riparian State. Art. 1 of the 1958 High Seas Convention unambiguously states that the term "high seas" means all parts of the sea that are not included in the territorial sea or in the internal waters of a State. In 1907 when Hague Convention No. XIII was drafted, sea areas where the coastal State exercised *droits souverains or juridiction* were synonymous with *eaux neutres* or *eaux territoriales*. In each case what was meant was what in modern terminology is called the territorial sea of the neutral State.[118]

This is, however, not the end of the problem. As long as the law of the sea undergoes revolutionary changes and the law of naval warfare does not, the two branches of international law must in one way or another be reconciled with each other. Whether this reconciliation process is called a process of analogy or adaptation does not matter. Thus the argument of a teleological nature that the exclusive economic zone with its *sui generis* legal status enjoys in times of war a neutrality *sui generis*, is deserving of careful and serious analysis.

One could even attempt to argue, for example, that in times of naval war the sovereign rights and other forms of national jurisdiction of the coastal State with respect to exploration and exploitation of natural

---

[117] Art. 31 par. 1 Law of Treaties.

[118] This result is corroborated by the Official Records of the Second Hague Peace Conference 1907, see, *Scott* (note 83), vol. I, 292 where the term "neutral jurisdiction" is used synonymously with "the neutral's territorial waters", and "violation of its sovereignty"; Art. 3 of Hague XIII speaks of "territorial waters" of a neutral power and in the next sentence uses the phrase that the ship "is within its jurisdiction"; Art. 5 uses the term "neutral waters", Art. 8 prefers the language "any vessel within its jurisdiction", while Art. 9 again uses "territorial waters".

resources, whether living or non-living, marine scientific research, or protection and preservation of the marine environment, should not be interfered with and, consequently, restrict the freedom of belligerent naval operations in the exclusive economic zone. This would be clearly in accordance with the intentions of those who favored a legal status of the economic zone close to or even identical with that of the territorial sea or who interpret the reservation of the exclusive economic zone for "peaceful purposes" as a *de jure* demilitarization of this 200 nautical miles zone.[119]

When considering these arguments, one should not lose sight of the all important fact, however, that the law of neutrality is a branch of the law of peace, which has only been modified by the state of war between other subjects of international law. The law of neutrality itself is not a constituent part of the law of war.[120] Taken in this context the position is untenable that in times of war belligerents may not operate in exclusive economic zones of third States. UNCLOS III refused to discuss any problems of the law of war or of the law of neutrality. This is clearly a matter not regulated by the new LOS Convention. According to its preamble,[121] those matters continue to be governed by the rules and principles of general international law. Furthermore, neutrality is an offspring of sovereignty, and Art. 58 par. 2 of the new LOS Convention makes Art. 89 applicable to the legal status of the exclusive economic zone, thus ensuring that no State may validly purport to subject any part of the waters concerned to its sovereignty. If this is true in time of peace, it amounts to a clear prohibition in time of war to attempt to subject the exclusive economic zone to principles of neutrality.[122]

This interaction and interdependence between sovereignty and neutrality is the basis of Hague XIII. As the Committee Report to the Second Hague Peace Conference put it: "The starting point of the regulations ought to be the sovereignty of the neutral State, which cannot be affected by the mere fact that a war exists in which it does not intend to participate ... The obligation, to respect the sovereignty of neutral States, is not a consequence of the war any more than the right of the State to inviolability of its territory is a consequence of its neutrality. As was said by *Sir Ernest Satow* in commenting upon an article of the British proposal, we have here 'the expression of the masterthought of this division of international law'."[123]

---

119 For this discussion, see, *Rauch* (note 91), 29—43.

120 *Berber* (note 93), 215.

121 Preamble, last paragraph.

122 A detailed discussion can be found in *Rauch* (note 91), 146—149.

123 *Scott* (note 83) vol. I, 288 *et seq.*; meeting of 27 July 1909.

In this respect the new LOS Convention is very clear: only internal waters, the territorial sea, and archipelagic waters belong to the territory of the coastal State, not so the exclusive economic zone. The principle of neutrality is applicable alike to land warfare and to naval warfare. The Regulations elaborated by the Second Hague Peace Conference on the subject of the rights and duties of neutral States on land begin with the provision: "The territory of neutral States is inviolable."[124] This corroborates the analysis of the rules concerning neutrality in naval war. It follows that acts of hostility between belligerents can be committed in the exclusive economic zones of neutral States as a legitimate exercise of traditional rights under the law of war. This includes not only hostilities properly so called, such as ship to ship combat, but also such operations of naval warfare as capture and the exercise of the right of visit and search.

4. International Straits

Security policy implications associated with straits transit, and in particular the concern for continued effectiveness and credibility of the submarine-based element of the so-called nuclear triad, made the straits regime one of the key sectors of the UNCLOS III negotiations and the new LOS Convention.

a) Transit Passage

The new transit passage regime is applicable only in straits used for international navigation.[125] In straits used for non-international navigation only unsuspendable innocent passage for merchant vessels and warships applies.[126] There are three exceptions as far as international straits are concerned: The legal regime in straits in which passage is regulated in whole or in part by long-standing international conventions in force specifically relating to such straits, prevails and is not altered by the Convention.[127] If the strait is formed by an island of a state bordering the strait and its mainland, the traditional regime of unsuspendable innocent passage applies if a route exists seaward of the island through the high seas or through the EEZ of similar convenience with respect to navigational and hydrographical characteristics.[128] And,

[124] Art. 1 Hague Convention V respecting the Rights and Duties of Neutral Powers and Persons in Case of War on Land; *Hinz/Rauch* (note 1), No. 1535; RGBl 1910, 151.

[125] Arts. 34, 36, 37.

[126] This is the consequence of Art. 34 par. 1.

[127] Art. 35 (c).

[128] Arts. 38 par. 1, 45 par. 1 (a).

finally, the regime of unsuspendable innocent passage applies in straits between a part of the high seas or an exclusive economic zone and the territorial sea of a foreign State.[129]

Transit passage means the exercise of the freedom of navigation and overflight solely for the purpose of continuous and expeditious transit of the strait between one part of the high seas or an exclusive economic zone and another part of the high seas or an exclusive economic zone.[130] This unsuspendable right is enjoyed by all ships and aircraft, including warships and military aircraft.[131] Ships and aircraft, while exercising the right of transit passage shall

— proceed without delay through or over the strait;

— refrain from any threat or use of force against the sovereignty, territorial integrity or political independence of States bordering the strait, or in any other manner in violation of the principles of international law embodied in the Charter of the United Nations;

— refrain from any activities other than those incident to their normal modes of continuous and expeditious transit unless rendered necessary by *force majeure* or by distress.[132]

The strait State may adopt limited and precisely circumscribed laws and regulations relating to transit passage in respect of the safety of navigation, prevention, reduction and control of pollution and the prevention of fishing and contravention of the customs, fiscal, immigration or sanitary laws and regulations.[133] The first two categories give the State only competence to incorporate international standards into his national laws. All four are subject to the requirement that they must not in their application have the practical effect of denying, hampering or impairing the right of transit passage.[134] It is noteworthy that there is no competence to adopt laws or regulations for security reasons. The regulatory and enforcement jurisdiction to prevent, reduce and control pollution of the marine environment does not affect the transit passage regime.[135] Warships and military aircraft have to comply with the above laws and regulations. However, if they act in a manner inconsistent with such laws and regulations the strait State may neither prevent transit passage nor require the ship or aircraft to leave the

[129] Art. 45 par. 1 (b).
[130] Art. 38 par. 2.
[131] Arts. 38 par. 1, 44.
[132] Art. 39 par. 1.
[133] Art. 42 par. 1.
[134] Art. 42 par. 2.
[135] Art. 233.

strait. It can only turn to the flag state which bears international responsibility for any loss or damage. This is a distinctly different feature compared with the innocent passage regime.[136]

This regime represents a carefully balanced compromise between the naval powers' vital interest in the high seas freedom of transit and the legitimate marine safety, pollution and resource interests of the strait State. It is a device to preserve in such international straits the freedom of navigation and overflight equivalent to a corridor of high seas through such straits without in any other respects affecting the legal status of the waters forming the strait. The right of transit passage is patterned after the high seas freedom of navigation and overflight and is juridically distinct from the right of innocent passage under the international law of the sea. In other words, the right of transit passage is a specific formulation of the high seas freedoms of navigation and overflight. This is corroborated by the negotiating history. The Conference rejected the proposal by a group of states to have innocent passage through the general territorial sea and straits transit treated as synonymous.[137] The question arises whether the new regime of transit passage, either upon the entry into force of the LOS Convention or after some lapse of time as customary international law under the law of peace, will have any influence on the law of naval warfare.

It might be useful in the analysis of this issue to reflect more closely at the situation which existed before UNCLOS III. Hague XIII does not address belligerent and neutral rights and duties in straits; the Hague Peace Conference of 1907 instead confined itself to codifying rules concerning the territorial sea in general, without making any distinction whatsoever between "ordinary" territorial sea and straits. Art. 10 of Hague XIII provides that the neutrality of a power is not affected by the mere passage through its territorial waters of warships or prizes belonging to belligerents. Art. 9 merely requires the neutral coastal State to apply impartially to belligerents the conditions, restrictions, or prohibitions made by it with regard to the admission into its territorial waters of belligerent warships or of their prizes.

The Hague Peace Conference of 1907 seems to have intentionally avoided specifically addressing the straits problem. In a meeting of

---

[136] Art. 42 par. 5 *versus* Arts. 25 par. 1, 30.

[137] See, UN Doc. A/AC. 138/SC. II/L. 18 of 27 March 1973; UN Doc. A/AC. 138/SC. II/SR. 60 of 4 April 1973, 188; Informal Spanish amendment of 30 March 1976, Art. 41, reprinted in: *Renate Platzöder*, Dokumente der Dritten Seerechtskonferenz der Vereinten Nationen, New Yorker Sessionen 1976, vol. II, Ebenhausen 1977, 522; Informal Greek amendment of 30 March 1976, Art. 39 par. 3, reprinted in: *op. cit.*, 530.

Committee III on 27 July 1907, the head of the Swedish delegation called attention to the special condition of straits which might be situated within an area of territorial waters and suggested the addition of a provision which had been voted by the Institut de Droit International in 1894: "Straits which serve as a passage from one open sea to another open sea can never be closed." The Danish delegate on 30 July 1907 explained an amendment, submitted by his delegation, according to which none of the provisions contained in the draft convention should be interpreted "so as to prohibit in time of war the mere passage through neutral waters joining two open seas by a warship or auxiliary ship of a belligerent".[138] The Committee Report mentions that the question was discussed without, however, any resolution being passed on this point.

From the opinions expressed it seemed that a neutral State may forbid even innocent passage through limited parts of its territorial waters so far as that was considered necessary to maintain its neutrality, but that this prohibition could not extend to straits uniting two open seas.[139] The language finally adopted in Art. 10 "does not touch at all upon the preceding questions, which are left under the empire of the general law of nations. It confines itself to saying that the passage through neutral territorial waters of warships or prizes belonging to belligerents does not affect the neutrality of the State, and thus implies at the same time that the belligerents do not contravene neutrality by passing and that the neutral does not fail in his duties by permitting them to pass."[140] At the subcommittee meeting of 30 Juli 1907 the Ottoman delegation declared that under the exceptional conditions created for the straits of the Dardanelles and the Bosporus by treaties in force, these straits, which are an integral part of Turkish territory, could in no case be brought within the scope of the treaty article. The Imperial Ottoman government could undertake no engagement whatsoever which would tend to limit its undoubted rights over these straits.[141] The Japanese delegation also declared that its government undertook no engagement concerning the straits which separate the numerous islands and islets composing the Japanese Empire and which are simply integral parts of the Empire.[142] The problems of the Ottoman delegation were later taken care of by the preamble of the Convention providing that the "following common rules" cannot modify provisions laid down in existing general treaties.[143]

---

[138] *Scott* (note 38) vol. I, 297, 298; see also, vol. III, 702 Annex 45.

[139] *Op. cit.*, vol. I, 298.

[140] *Ibid.*

[141] *Op. cit.* vol. III, 599; see also, vol. I, 298.

[142] *Op. cit.* vol. I, 298.

[143] See, the last paragraph of the preamble.

In the final analysis there was just one delegation (Japan) at the 1907 Hague Peace Conference which harbored some doubts about the freedom of passage of belligerent warships through straits bordered by neutral countries. As for the legal quality of this right of passage, the statement of Mr. *Haggerup,* delegate of Norway, is of importance. He said that "in territorial waters innocent passage of vessels is permitted even in time of war".[144] There was no objection to this statement in the Committee or in Plenary.

The point of view of the overwhelming majority of States participating at the Hague Conference of 1907 is corroborated by State practice. During the Crimean War 1854—56, the Franco-Prussian War 1871, the Russo-Turkish War 1877—78 and the Russo-Japanese War 1904—05, Denmark and Sweden allowed belligerent warships to pass freely through the Sound and the Belts.[145] During the Crimean War Denmark expressly refused to accede to a British request that the straits be closed to belligerent warships.[146] The neutrality laws of Denmark and Sweden, promulgated in 1912, excluded from the territorial waters which might be closed to foreign warships in time of war those portions of the straits indispensable to the passage of ships.[147] Under political pressure from Germany, however, and in order to protect its territory, Denmark mined the two Belts and its part of the Sound during World War I and prohibited the passage of warships. At day time merchant vessels were led through the minefields under pilotage.[148] In World War I Chile claimed the straits of Magellan to be within its territorial waters but did allow unimpeded passage of warships.[149] On 27 May 1938 Denmark, Finland, Iceland, Norway, and Sweden concluded an Agreement regarding Similar Rules of Neutrality.[150] Based upon this treaty the two riparian States of the Baltic approaches promulgated rules of neutrality which authorized belligerent vessels in time of war to transit through the "natural routes of traffic between the North Sea and the Baltic Sea".[151]

---

[144] *Scott* (note 83) vol. III, 617.

[145] *Erik Brüel,* International Straits: A Treatise on International Law, Copenhagen 1947, vol. II, 55, 56; vol. I, 111; *Herbert Arthur Smith* (ed.), Great Britain and the Law of Nations, vol. II, London 1935, 262—267.

[146] *Smith* (note 145), 262.

[147] *Francis Deák/Philip C. Jessup,* A Collection of Neutrality Laws, Regulations and Treaties of Various Countries, vol. I, Washington D.C. 1939, 476 and 963.

[148] *Brüel* (note 145) vol. II, 59—78.

[149] *Op. cit.*, 249.

[150] LNTS vol. 188 (1938), 193.

[151] Danish Royal Ordinance No. 209 of 31 May 1938, *op. cit.*, 297; Swedish Royal Ordinance No. 187 of 27 May 1938, *ibid.*

Differing positions, however, in fact existed with respect to the Sound and the Belts. Sweden, during World War II exercised the right of visit and search of German merchant vessels passing through the Flint Channel between the island of Saltholm and Malmö in the Sound. Further, upon request of the German Supreme Command of the Danish coasts, the Foreign Office in Berlin on 6 June 1940 issued a secret legal memorandum which read in part: "It might be possible to argue that under international law doctrine and according to the opinion expressed by many States at the 1930 Hague Codification Conference a strait which like the Sound connects two open seas is free for navigation and not subject to restrictions or control as long as the coastal State is neutral. This principle has been shared by Germany in negotiations before the war. Today, however, this principle can barely be considered as a recognized rule of international law, since the Lausanne Convention of 1923 which represented the main precedent of the claim for extensive freedom of navigation in straits, has been replaced by the Montreux Convention, which heavily stresses the sovereignty of the coastal State over a strait. In addition, Germany itself during the war has taken the position that the closing of straits by the riparian States is possible. The latter information is added for top secret information of the commander only. In view of this situation it is impossible to base the claim for unimpeded passage of German merchant ships through the Sound against Sweden on customary international law or on treaty law."[152]

Such a position, however, seems to be rather an exception. The straits of Gibraltar were freely used as an avenue of approach for warships during the invasion of North Africa in World War II.[153] Denmark and Sweden have several times amended their legislation concerning the admission of foreign warships and military aircraft to their territory, in each instance recognizing a more liberal passage regime through straits as opposed to general territorial waters. The Danish Royal Ordinance of 27 February 1976 applies when Denmark as well as the flag State of the vessel or aircraft are in a state of peace, and the ordinance is therefore of no direct interest in this context. An unsuspended right of innocent passage, without need for notification, is recognized in the Danish portion of the Sound.[154] The Swedish Royal Notice No. 366 of 3 June 1966 concerning the Admission to Swedish Territory of foreign Warships and military Aircraft[155] provides that

---

[152] Urkunden zum Seekriegsrecht (note 70), No. 432.

[153] *Samuel Eliot Morison*, History of United States Naval Operations in World War II, vol. II: Operations in North African Waters, October 1942 — June 1943, London 1947, 191.

[154] See, Art. 1, in: UNLS, National Legislation and Treaties relating to the Law of the Sea, New York 1980 (UN Doc. ST/LEG/SER. B/19), 142.

Notice No. 366 shall cease to have effect only if Sweden becomes a belligerent in a war, thereby making clear that the Notice applies to wartime situations when Sweden is not a party to the conflict. The Notice contains stipulations which become effective only when the King so orders. These special provisions include an article to the effect that warships of a belligerent power shall be admitted to the territorial sea of Sweden for the purpose of passage not to exceed a period of twenty-four successive hours. Passage through the territorial sea by submarines and hovercraft, however, is permitted only in the Sound between the lines Kullen-Gilbjerghoved and Cape Falsterbo-Stevns light.[156] Military aircraft of a belligerent power shall, for the purpose of passage without unnecessary deviations of course, be admitted to the airspace above the territorial sea in the Sound between the same lines.[157] The same restrictions apply for foreign vessels captured by a belligerent power for the purpose of passage through the Sound.[158]

Taken together, doctrine and State practice would seem to justify the conclusion that if the littoral States are neutral, innocent passage of belligerent warships through international straits in time of war may be interfered with only in exceptional cases. The situation is, of course, different if the strait States are at war. As belligerents, their territorial waters are part of the theater of war and, in principle, the strait State is entitled to all belligerent rights against the enemy's fleet and against his seaborne commerce, including visit and search, contraband control, *etc.* It follows that the belligerent strait State may attack enemy ships in the strait and destroy them, seize contraband, capture neutral ships guilty of rendering unneutral service to the enemy, and so forth. Thus enemy ships will be denied passage and enemy vessels as well as neutral vessels are subject to the same treatment as on the high seas. The adverse party may, by the same token, wage war against the strait State in its territorial waters. Exceptions, of course, exist.

An all-encompassing blockade of an international strait, *e. g.* by mines, is prohibited.[159] As far as passage of neutral ships, particularly warships, is concerned, the International Court of Justice (ICJ) rendered a noteworthy judgment in the Corfu Channel case. On 22 October 1946 a

---

[155] UNLS, National Legislation and Treaties Relating to the Territorial Sea, the Contiguous Zone, the Continental Shelf, the High Seas and to Fishing and Conservation of the Living Resources of the Sea, New York 1970 (UN Doc. ST/LEG/SER. B/15), 259.

[156] Art. 16.

[157] Art. 18.

[158] Art. 27.

[159] US Draft Law of Naval Operations, NWP 10—1, Part I Chapter 2, Section 2.3.8.25, issued 6 July 1982.

squadron of British warships proceeded through the strait of Corfu, and in the course of the transit, two destroyers struck mines and were heavily damaged, with deaths and injuries among the crew. Previously, British warships had been fired upon in the strait and Albania and the United Kingdom had accused each other of violating international law. The ICJ rendered three judgments. In the second judgment of 4 April 1949, it noted that the minefield which had caused the damage and losses had been recently laid by Albania and that Albania and Greece were considered to be technically in a state of war. The ICJ held that Albania would have been justified in issuing regulations regarding passage of warships through the Corfu Channel, "but not in prohibiting such passage or in subjecting it to the requirement of special authorization".[160] If the Corfu Channel judgment can be interpreted as applying to warships in time of war, the ramifications include that a belligerent strait State is obliged not to obstruct innocent passage by neutrals subject to reasonable measures of security and control.[161]

UNCLOS III gave birth to the regime of transit passage through international straits, including submerged passage and overflight. In other words, the new LOS Convention permits continuous and expeditious transit of ships and aircraft operating in their normal modes[162] through these bottlenecks of international navigation.[163] In the aftermath of UNCLOS III, the question arises whether under the new regime a neutral strait State may prohibit belligerent transit of warships or military aircraft, or, if the strait State is a party to the conflict, whether it is entitled to restrict the transit passage of vessels and aircraft of neutral States. There are two considerations that strongly suggest a negative answer: the legal quality of the transit passage right and the scope of application of the straits chapter in the new LOS Convention.

As has been pointed out, the right of transit passage is patterned after the high seas freedom of navigation and its juridically distinct from the right of innocent passage under the traditional law of the sea, which never included submerged passage or overflight.[164] In other words, the right of transit passage is a specific formulation of the high seas freedom of navigation and overflight. This formulation, a condition *sine qua non* for the naval powers, is by no means an onslaught on the sovereignty of the strait States. Just the opposite. One of the advantages of

---

[160] ICJ Reports 1949, 12.

[161] *R. R. Baxter*, Passage of ships through international waterways in time of war, in: BYIL vol. 31 (1954), 189—216 (204).

[162] For the interpretation of this term, see, *supra*, 27—30 and note 91.

[163] Art. 38.

[164] See, Art. 14 of the 1958 Convention on the Territorial Sea and the Contiguous Zone.

the new transit passage concept is that it keeps the littoral States bordering straits with great strategic value out of the vicious circle of escalation in times of tension and crisis.[165] If transit through such straits were subject to the discretion of the coastal States, they would unavoidably become involved, even if the discretionary power were to be exercised evenhandedly, *i. e.*, even if they meticulously abided by the rule that all restrictions or prohibitions have to be applied impartially to the belligerents.[166] The ramifications of a refusal or of a permission of transit in whole or in part — *e. g.*, only surface navigation, or surface and submerged navigation, or navigation and overflight — could, albeit legally non-discriminatory, in fact be of quite different military and strategic value to the parties to the conflict. Depending upon the geographical situation or geopolitical implications, the same decision might be considered as a friendly or an unfriendly act by differently situated belligerents. Under the transit passage regime of the new LOS Convention, this potentially destabilizing discretion is withheld, with no room for permission requirements or prohibitions by strait States at all. The escalation-preventing quality of transit passage in times of tension and crisis — *i. e.* in times of fragile peace — are even more important for neutral strait States in times of armed conflict.

I will not touch here upon the question of the viability of the very concept of neutrality in light of the collective security system established by the United Nations Charter.[167] If this concept as such, however, is to have any meaning at all in future naval conflicts, it will have to be adjusted to take into account the new developments in the law of the sea. And as far as transit passage through straits is concerned, the law of neutrality has to reflect the new and delicate balance that has been struck and must conform with the accommodation of the security interests of the strait States and the navigational interests of all other States, including the naval powers.

It is not only such a teleological approach that leads one to the conclusion that under the legal regime of the new LOS Convention the recognition of belligerent transit rights through neutral straits used for international navigation, including submerged transit and overflight through the superjacent airspace, is a necessity. It must also be considered that the transit passage regime is not restricted to those straits which are overlapped by a 12 nautical miles territorial sea. It no longer holds true that straits in a geographical sense only become straits in

---

165 *Elmar Rauch*, Militärische Aspekte der Seerechtsentwicklung, in: *Wolfgang Graf Vitzthum* (ed.), Aspekte der Seerechtsentwicklung, München 1980, 75—125.

166 Art. 8 Hague Convention XIII.

167 See, *Robert W. Tucker*, The Law of War and Neutrality at Sea, Washington 1957, 171, 180.

a legal sense when the territorial seas of the coastal State or States meet or overlap. If straits used for international navigation within the meaning of the new LOS Convention were nothing more than a geographically specific stretch of territorial sea, the concept of sovereignty as the fundamental basis for the very idea of neutrality might not be overcome by the impact of the law of the sea developments. Such is not the case, however, although the wrong impression seems to prevail that a strait by definition is overlapped by two bands of water representing areas of coastal State sovereignty, subject only to special exceptions.

The new LOS Convention does not define the term "strait". For want of a composite definition, one has to extract the meaning from a number of discrete treaty articles. The very first provision of Part III on straits dealing with the legal status of waters forming international straits makes reference to the exercise by the States bordering straits of their sovereignty "or jurisdiction" over such waters and their airspace, seabed and subsoil.[168] Sovereignty is exercised exclusively in the territorial sea.[169] Jurisdictional zones are the contiguous zone[170] and the exclusive economic zone,[171] and as far as the seabed and subsoil is concerned, the continental shelf.[172] The above mentioned treaty provision, therefore, presupposes international straits of a greater width than 24 nautical miles. The article defining the scope of Part III goes even further in declaring that nothing in that Part affects the legal status of the waters beyond the territorial seas of States bordering straits as exclusive economic zones or high seas.[173] That means there can be straits formed even by high seas waters.

I shall not examine in this context the issue of whether there is a difference between the continental shelf regime and the exclusive economic zone, in that the rights of the coastal State over the continental shelf do not depend upon an express proclamation,[174] while an exclusive economic zone may have to be claimed expressly like the territorial sea. If the economic zone is assimilated to the continental shelf approach the LOS Convention may under certain circumstances include more than 400 nautical miles wide narrows in the straits concept. Art. 36 of the LOS Convention spells out the consequences of this aspect of the straits part. The meaning of Art. 36, unfortunately, is easier to grasp if one articulates it in affirmative terminology, rather

168 Art. 34.
169 Art. 2.
170 Art. 33.
171 Art. 56; see, *supra*, 33—38.
172 Art. 76.
173 Art. 35 (b).
174 Art. 77 par. 3.

than couched in the negative terms preferred by the drafters. In short, the regime of transit passage applies even if a high seas route or an economic zone route through the strait exist, so long as such routes, when compared to a route through the bordering territorial seas, are not of similar convenience with respect to navigational and hydrographical characteristics.

In times of peace, military aircraft flying at high speed may not be in a position to follow a turning and twisting band of high seas or economic zone between two territorial seas in a strait. Such aircraft would thus have the right of transit passage under the LOS Convention and may transit through the airspace over the territorial seas of the strait States. A strategic submarine trying to stay submerged in order to avoid detection by a surveillance satellite of an potential enemy might also not be able to navigate safely between the territorial seas of the strait States, due to shallow waters or other oceanographic features existent in the high sea or economic zone channels. The submarine could thus transit in a submerged mode through the territorial seas of the coastal States.

If the traditional rules of neutrality were applied in a mechanical fashion to the cases covered by Art. 36 of the new LOS Convention, the huge submarines of one party to the conflict would have to navigate on the surface because of safety reasons, while smaller submarines of the enemy could pass unnoticed through the strait where the limited depth of a high seas channel allowed. Or, at low speed, an aircraft might be able to follow the winding economic zones corridor between the airspace over the territorial seas of the strait States, but at the expense of becoming more vulnerable to certain ship-to-air missiles of the enemy. The mere possibility of a strait State imposing such mix-and-match distinctions and thereby interfering with transit passage in time of war would inevitably involve such a State in one way or another in the conflict. Too much would already depend on geographic, oceanographic, hydrographic, and navigational circumstances, and the very notion of neutrality would seem to require that a neutral State, in order to safeguard its impartiality, should not attempt to interpose itself regarding transit of merchant ships or warships, including warships of the belligerents.

In summary, the peace time LOS Convention regime of transit passage is tantamount to a belligerent transit right through neutral straits in times of war. It might be mentioned that the requirement for transit passage to be exercised continuously and expeditiously[175] matches perfectly with the basic idea underlying the 24-hour rule contained in Art. 12 of the

[175] Art. 38 par. 2.

Hague Convention No. XIII. In the aftermath of UNCLOS III, Art. 10 of Hague XIII has to be construed as meaning that the neutrality of a power is not affected by the belligerent right of continuous, expeditious, and unobstructed transit passage through straits used for international navigation.

b) Long-Standing Treaty Regime

To be sure, the adaptation of the law of neutrality in armed conflict at sea to the LOS developments has to take into consideration the exceptions applicable to the transit passage regime. No difficulties are created by the exceptions pertaining to straits which are formed by an island or a State bordering the strait and its mainland[176] and by straits between a part of the high seas or an exclusive economic zone and the territorial sea of a foreign State.[177] In such straits the traditional regime of nonsuspendable innocent passage applies.[178] This is a mere reaffirmation of the existing law.[179] Hence it follows that the law of neutrality in naval warfare should remain unchanged as well.

A third exception from the transit passage regime concerns those straits in which passage is regulated in whole or in part by long-standing international conventions in force specifically relating to such straits.[180] Transit passage does not affect the legal regime in such straits. This exception, which clearly applies to the Montreux Convention, has the problem of inviting a proliferation of additional claimants seeking exempted status based on far less convincing arguments concerning various historical treaties. This may lead to significant legal uncertainties in certain straits about the appropriate regime of passage, both in time of peace as well as in time of armed conflict. As an example, *John Norton Moore*, former United States Ambassador to UNCLOS III and former chairman of the National Security Council Interagency Task Force on the Law of the Sea headed the US team that participated in the development of the navigation and security aspects of the Informal Single Negotiating Text of UNCLOS III. He has subsequently written that in his opinion, this category of straits includes, in addition to the Turkish Straits, the Danish Straits and the Strait of Magellan.[181] This opinion is shared by a former high ranking military expert

176 Art. 38 par. 1.

177 Art. 45 par. 1 (b).

178 Art. 45.

179 Art. 16 par. 4 of the 1958 Convention on the Territorial Sea and the Contiguous Zone.

180 Art. 35 (c).

181 *Moore* (note 91), 111.

in the USSR delegation to UNCLOS III, *General Pjotr Barabolja.*[182] Furthermore, the delegations of Denmark, Sweden and Finland claimed time and again during the UNCLOS III negotiations that this treaty exception applied not only to the Belts and the Sound in the so-called Danish Straits, but also to the Alands-Hav between Sweden and the Aland Islands in the Baltic.[183]

Despite the total silence of the official records concerning these matters, there seem to have been secret negotiations (with mixed reports as to the outcome) between the superpowers and a number of important straits States. It is revealing that the representative of Denmark at least two times stated for the record that "after negotiations with all interested parties his delegation was satisfied that Art. 35 (c) applied to the specific regime in the Danish straits".[184] There is no record of these negotiations or of the possible understandings which may have been reached, but we must in any event disregard such corridor consultations, since they could never change, in particular not counter the ordinary meaning of the black letter text in its LOS treaty context and in the light of its object and purpose.[185]

Passage is "regulated" within the meaning of Art. 35 (c) of the LOS Convention in the Montreux Convention, signed 20 July 1936, concerning the Bosporus and the Dardanelles.[186] This Convention contains detailed rules and regulations on the passage of merchant vessels and warships in time of peace and in time of war. In time of peace, merchant

[182] Modernes Seevölkerrecht, published by the Academy of Science of the USSR, translated into German by *Elmar Rauch*, vol. 1, Baden-Baden 1978, 230.

[183] Sweden — UN Doc. A/CONF. 62/SR. 163 of 6 April 1982, 3; UN Doc. A/CONF. 62/SR. 136 of 26 August 1980, 15; Denmark — UN Doc. A/CONF. 62/SR. 138 of 26 August 1980, 35, and UN Doc. A/CONF. 62/SR. 163 of 6 April 1982, 10; Finland — UN Doc. A/CONF. 62/SR. 135 of 25 August 1980, 8.

[184] UN Doc. A/CONF. 62/SR. 138 of 26 August 1980, 35; UN Doc. A/CONF. 62/SR. 163 of 6 April 1982, 10.

[185] Insofar I am in total agreement with *Michael Reismann* (note 91); however, he is wrong with respect to the term "normal mode" as used in the LOS Convention. In my opinion this result cannot be influenced by the fact that *John Norton Moore*, who headed the US team that participated in the development of the transit passage regime provisions has subsequently written that in his opinion this category of straits includes besides the Turkish Straits, the Danish Straits and the Strait of Magellan, see, *Moore* (note 91), 111; this view is shared by the former ranking military expert on the USSR delegation to UNCLOS III, *Major General Pjotr D. Barabolja*, in: *M. J. Lazarew*, Sovremennoe Meždunarodnoe Morskoe Pravo. Režim vod i dna mirovogo okeana (Contemporary International Law of the Sea. The Regime of the Waters and the Seabed of the World Ocean), Moskau 1974, 84; German translation by *Rauch* (note 182), 105; see also, *Pjotr Barabolja/D. Uzonov*, Problema meždunarodnych prolivov na III konferencii OON po morskomu pravu (The problem of international straits at the Third UN Law of the Sea Conference), in: Morskoj sbornik 1977, No. 8, 95 *et seq.*

[186] LNTS vol. 173 (1936—37), 213.

vessels enjoy complete freedom of transit and navigation in the Straits, by day and by night, under any flag and with any kind of cargo. In time of war, Turkey not being belligerent, merchant vessels, under any flag or with any kind of cargo, enjoy freedom of transit and navigation in the Straits. When Turkey is at war, merchant vessels not belonging to a country at war with Turkey enjoy freedom of transit and navigation in the Straits on condition that they do not in any way assist the enemy. Such vessels shall enter the Straits by day and their transit shall be effected by the route which shall in each case be indicated by the Turkish authorities.[187]

As far as warships are concerned, the Montreux Convention sets forth in Annex II the definitions of vessels of war and of their specification (capital ships, aircraft carriers, light surface vessels, submarines, minor war vessels, and auxiliary vessels). In time of peace, light surface vessels, minor war vessels and auxiliary vessels, whether belonging to Black Sea or non-Black Sea powers, and whatever their flag, enjoy freedom of transit through the Straits subject to prior notification and certain restrictions with respect to tonnage. Black Sea powers may send through the Straits capital ships up to a certain tonnage without restrictions, provided that these vessels pass through singly, escorted by not more than two destroyers. Black Sea powers also have the right to send through, for the purpose of joining their base, submarines constructed or purchased outside the Black Sea, provided that adequate notice of the construction or purchase of such submarines shall have been given to Turkey. Submarines belonging to said powers shall also be entitled to pass through the Straits to be repaired in dockyards outside the Black Sea, on condition that detailed information on the matter is given to Turkey. In either case, the submarines must travel by day and on the surface, and must pass through the Straits singly.[188]

In time of war, Turkey not being belligerent, neutral warships enjoy complete freedom of transit through the Straits under the same conditions as during peacetime. Warships of belligerents are prohibited from transiting the Straits. Exceptions are made if the warship is assisting in the defense of a State linked with Turkey by a mutual assistance treaty, is carrying out obligations under the Covenant of the League of Nations, or is returning to base from which it has become separated. When Turkey is at war these provisions are not applicable, and the passage of warships is left entirely to the discretion of the Turkish government.[189]

---

[187] Arts. 1, 2, 4, 5 of the Montreux Convention.

[188] Arts. 8, 10, 11, 12, 13—18 of the Montreux Convention.

[189] Arts. 10, 20, 25 of the Montreux Convention.

In contrast, the Treaty for the Redemption of the Sound Dues of 14 March 1857,[190] whatever might be claimed by the delegations of Sweden, Denmark and Finland, does not "regulate" passage at all, neither in whole nor in part. The treaty merely makes indirect reference to freedom of navigation under customary international law. I have thoroughly analyzed this treaty elsewhere and will restrict myself to this general statement here.[191]

Art. 5 of the Convention Respecting the Non-Fortification and Neutralization of the Aland Islands provides simply that the prohibition on warships entering or remaining in the neutrality zone does not restrict the freedom of innocent passage through the territorial waters; such passage remains subject to existing international rules and usages.[192] Rumor has it that the fact that the Aland neutrality zone covers only about half of the Alands Hav led to the insertion of the phrase "regulated in whole 'or in part' " in Art. 35 (c) of the LOS Convention. Unless one is to throw overboard all rules of treaty interpretation as codified in the Vienna Convention on the Law of Treaties, however, it is impossible to construe Art. 5 of the Aland Convention as a treaty provision "regulating" passage through the strait.

Neither is passage through the straits of Magellan "regulated" by the Boundary Treaty between Argentina and Chile, signed 23 July 1881. Its Art. V only contains a reference to the free navigation of the strait by the ships of all nations.[193] There is nothing more to it.

If the points of view expressed by Denmark, Sweden and Finland at UNCLOS III were correct, then also the Strait of Gibraltar could be argued to qualify as a strait in which passage is "regulated in part" by a longstanding international convention, because the Declaration respecting Egypt and Morocco, signed 8 April 1904 in London, contains a reference to free passage in connection with a prohibition on fortifications.[194] The same would apply to the Strait of Formosa because of the identical verbal notes of the French, German and Russian Ministers to the Japanese Foreign Minister regarding Retrocession of the Liaotung Peninsula, dated 18 October 1895.[195] In this case, however, the question

---

[190] *Clive Parry* (ed.), The Consolidated Treaty Series, Dobbs Ferry 1969—1981, vol. 116, 357 *et seq.; Geo. Fréd. de Martens,* Nouveau Recueil de Traités, vol. XVI, 2, Goettingen 1842, 345.

[191] *Rauch* (note 105), 81—86, 289—293 and 305, note 101.

[192] LNTS vol. 9 (1922), 212.

[193] *Geo. Fréd. de Martens,* Nouveau Recueil Général de Traités, 2nd seriés, contd. by *Felix Stoerck,* vol. XII, Göttingen 1887, 491.

[194] *Op. cit.* vol. XXXII, Leipzig 1905, 18.

[195] *John A. MacMurray,* Treaties and Agreements with and concerning China 1894—1919, vol. I, New York 1921, 53.

whether this treaty is still in force within the meaning of Art. 35 (c) of the LOS Convention would require further scrutiny.

In summary, the right of belligerent transit passage through straits used for international navigation is not applicable to the Turkish Straits, due to the clearly applicable exception in Art. 35 (c) of the LOS Convention and the Montreux Convention of 1936. Other would-be claimants to Art. 35 (c) status simply fail to make a credible case.

5. Archipelagic Sea Lanes

The new LOS Convention accepts the archipelagic concept, but only with an important rider, that of archipelagic sea lanes passage which, for all intents and purposes, can in this context be compared with the transit passage regime through international straits. In these sea lanes through archipelagos all States enjoy the freedom of passage, which means the rights of navigation and overflight in the normal mode solely for the purpose of continuous, expeditious and unobstructed transit.[196]

Such sea lanes and air routes shall be defined by a series of continuous axis lines from the entry points of all normal international passage routes through to the exit points. Ships and aircraft exercising archipelagic sea lanes passage shall not deviate more than 25 nautical miles to either side of such axis lines. Thus the new LOS Convention creates 50 nautical miles wide corridors through waters under the sovereignty of the archipelagic States.[197]

What has been said in connection with transit passage through straits applies *mutatis mutandis* to archipelagic sea lane passage, *i. e.*, in case of naval war, belligerents enjoy the freedom of transit including surface transit, submerged passage, and overflight through a neutral archipelago.

6. Deep Sea Bed and Ocean Floor

Part XI of the new LOS Convention creates the so-called "Area", which is defined as the sea-bed and ocean floor and subsoil thereof beyond the limits of national jurisdiction.[198] National jurisdiction on the sea-bed extends to the outer edge of the continental margin, as defined in Art. 76 of the Convention. The Area and its resources are the common heritage of mankind.[199] Neither the LOS Convention in general nor any

---

[196] Art. 53 par. 3.

[197] Art. 53 par. 5.

[198] Art. 1 par. 1, Arts. 133—191.

[199] Art. 136.

rights to explore and exploit the natural resources of the Area granted or exercised pursuant to Part XI affect the legal status of the waters superjacent to the Area or that of the air space above those waters.[200]

Consequently, there are no restrictions on the traditional freedoms of the high seas, including the right to wage war in the water column, on the surface, or in the airspace over the Area. As for the Area itself, the Convention regulates only "activities" in this part of the sea-bed and ocean floor, which means all activities of exploration for, and exploitation of, the resources of the Area.[201] In other words, military uses in peace time and belligerent uses in time of war are not affected. This interpretation is corroborated by other portions of the LOS Convention, under which no State shall claim or exercise sovereignty or sovereign rights over any part of the Area. Nor shall any State or natural or juridical person appropriate any part thereof. No such claim or exercise of sovereignty or sovereign rights nor such appropriation shall be recognized.[202] The law of naval warfare remains unchanged as far as the new international Area is concerned.

7. Self-Defense in Neutral Waters

After the concept of coastal State sovereignty over an adjacent belt of water (the territorial sea) had been accepted, the famous Dutch jurist *Cornelis van Bynkershoek* in his book *"De dominio maris"* in 1703 suggested that this sovereignty extended only to the distance that a cannonball could travel, because the area beyond that could not be dominated and controlled from land. Since at that time a cannonball could cover only a distance of 3 nautical miles, this width of the territorial sea became customary.[203] This idea of power and control from land was the foundation of the very concept of territorial waters. In time of war, the neutral State had under all circumstances the means to enforce its neutrality and to prevent any abuse or violation of its neutrality by the belligerents.

With the development of new and ever more sophisticated methods and means of naval warfare, the problem of the weak or unwilling neutral arose. This problem has been tremendously exacerbated by developments in the law of the sea such as the extension of the territorial

---

[200] Art. 135.

[201] Art. 134 par. 2, Art. 1 par. 1 subpar. 3.

[202] Art. 137 par. 1.

[203] *Ian Brownlie*, Principles of Public International Law, 3rd ed., Oxford 1979, 183—185; *Charles Rousseau*, Droit international public, vol. IV: Les relations internationales, Paris 1980, 362—363.

sea to 12 nautical miles, and the recognition of archipelagic waters, archipelagic sea lanes and transit passage through international straits. Two examples of situations that could cause difficulty would be if (i) an enemy ballistic missile submarine attempted to take refuge in an international strait, or (ii) a party to the conflict attempted to use one of the huge archipelagos in the Pacific as a submarine sanctuary.

The Treaty of Washington of 8 May 1870 between the United States of America and Great Britain provided in Rule 3 of Article 6 that a neutral government is bound to exercise due diligence in its own ports and waters, and as to all persons within its jurisdiction, to prevent any violation of the obligation not to permit or suffer either belligerent to make use of its ports or waters as the base of naval operations against the other.[204] This principle met with no opposition at the Second Hague Peace Conference in 1907; a formula was merely sought which would not impose upon neutrals too heavy a responsibility in proportion to the means they had at their disposal.[205] This aim was achieved by the following wording of Art. 25 of Hague XIII: "A neutral Power is bound to exercise such surveillance as the means at its disposal allow to prevent any violation of the provisions of the above articles occuring in its ports or roadsteads or in its waters."

Two legal repercussions are clear in connection with the example scenarios mentioned above. The belligerent using the territorial sea or an archipelago of a neutral State as a "submarine sanctuary" would be committing a gross violation of Art. 5 of Hague XIII, since its warships would be using these neutral waters as a "base of naval operations against the adversary". That a weak neutral might not be able to procure modern surveillance equipment to prevent such violations does not constitute a violation of international law. He is protected by the *nemo ultra posse obligatur* proviso in the law of neutrality at sea.

The more delicate question concerns the legitimate options available to the other belligerent power. Hague XIII does not expressly forbid a belligerent to resort to acts of hostility in neutral waters against enemy vessels making illegal use of such waters, if a neutral State will not or can not effectively enforce its rights against such offending belligerent forces.[206] Nevertheless, some scholarly writers assert that the belligerent right of "self-help" against the naval forces of an enemy violating neutral rights does not extend to the exercise of hostile acts within neutral waters.[207] The United States Manual of Naval Warfare, however,

---

[204] *Scott* (note 83) vol. III, 597, 605.

[205] *Op. cit.*, 194.

[206] US LNW (note 54), No. 441.

[207] *Josef L. Kunz*, Kriegsrecht und Neutralitätsrecht, Wien 1935, 240.

states that it is recognized that when the means at the disposal of a neutral are clearly inadequate to fulfil its neutral obligations, a belligerent is not forbidden from taking, as an extreme measure, acts of hostility in neutral waters against an enemy making improper use of such neutrality.[208]

I suspect that in view of the strategic importance of the sea-borne element of the nuclear triad for the fragile balance of mutual deterrence, the law of naval warfare in the aftermath of UNCLOS III will develop along the lines of the law of warfare on land. Interestingly, in land warfare the neutral's duty has never been limited merely to using the means at its disposal. According to the Hague Convention V Respecting the Rights and Duties of Neutral Powers and Persons in Case of War on Land, a neutral power must not allow any violations of its neutrality to occur on its territory.[209] Should the neutral State be unable, or for any reason fail, to prevent violations of its neutrality by the troops of one belligerent entering or passing through its territory, the other belligerent may be justified in attacking the enemy forces on this territory.[210]

Many uncertainties remain, from the question of the legality of surveillance missions in neutral waters to the question of a preemptive strike against an enemy warship violating neutral waters. I shall come back to these questions in my concluding remarks.

---

[208] US LNW (note 54), note 27 for Chapter 4.

[209] Art. 5; see also, Arts. 6—15.

[210] US Dept. of the Army, The Law of Land Warfare, Washington 1956, Field Manual FM 27—10, No. 520. For this potential development of the law of naval warfare it seems of considerable importance that a new principle — unknown in western international law doctrince — recently surfaced in Soviet scholarly writings, the "legal principle of equal security of states in military navigation". This "fundamental norm of contemporary international law" is based mainly on the bilateral treaties and agreements between the Soviet Union and the United States, concluded in 1972, notably the Agreement on the Prevention of Incidents on and over the High Seas of 25 May 1972. See, Sovremennoe Meždunarodnoe Morskoe Pravo. Naučnye issledovanija. Ochrana morskoj sredy. Torgovoe i voennoe moreplavanie (Contemporary International Law of the Sea. Scientific Research. Protection of the Marine Environment. Merchant and Military Navigation), 253—260; German translation by *Rauch* (note 182), vol. 2, Baden-Baden 1981, 265—270.

IV. Scope of Application of Protocol I

Protocol I in many aspects directly and expressly regulates armed conflict at sea. It deals with the shipwrecked,[211] includes the conveyance by water in the term "medical transportation",[212] improves the protection of hospital ships and other medical ships and craft,[213] regulates the use of medical aircraft over sea areas[214] and preserves the generally recognized rules of international law applicable to the use of flags in the conduct of armed conflict at sea.[215] The main question, however, is whether the new rules for the protection of the civilian population, contained in Section I of Part IV (Art. 48—67), are applicable to naval war, and if so, to what extent.

1. Textual Interpretation of Art. 49

In this respect the scope of application of Protocol I is defined in Art. 49 par. 3 and 4:

— Paragraph 3 reads as follows: "The provisions of Section I of Part IV apply to any land, air or sea warfare, which may affect the civilian population, individual civilians or civilian objects on land. They further apply to all attacks against objectives on land but do not otherwise affect the rules of international law applicable in armed conflict at sea or in the air."

— Paragraph 4 is couched in the following terms: "The provisions of this Section are additional to the rules concerning humanitarian protection contained in the Fourth Convention ... and in other international agreements binding upon the High Contracting Parties, as well as to other rules of international law relating to the protection of civilians and civilian objects on land, at sea or in the air against the effects of hostilities."

This is a troublesome delineation indeed and seems to be open to differing or even contradictory interpretation. Since the term "attack" is the key word of the whole Section and Art. 49 jointly defines the

---

211 Art. 8 (b); see also, Art. 8 (e), Art. 9, Art. 10.

212 Art. 8 (f).

213 Art. 8 (i), Arts. 22, 23.

214 Arts. 24—31.

215 Art. 39 par. 3; see, *supra*, 24—27.

term attack and the scope of application, one feels inclined to take the last sentence of Art. 49 par. 3 as the starting point of any interpretative effort, despite the introductory words. This approach makes the most sense from a consistency of interpretation standpoint. The provisions of this Section would therefore apply to attacks from the sea against military objectives on land, but otherwise the rules of naval warfare remain untouched. In more concrete terms, this would mean that Protocol I prevails over Hague Convention IX of October 1907 concerning Bombardment by Naval Forces in Times of War.

However, the civilian population, individual civilians, and even objects (*e. g.*, animals) on land are by no means only affected by bombardments by naval forces. In both World Wars this kind of bombardment was rather negligible and the effects of naval blockades and contraband control were far more important and had greater ramifications on the everyday life of millions of people in continental Europe. The object and purpose of Protocol I — to improve the protection of the civilian population in international armed conflicts — seem to require a more comprehensive scope of application. As a matter of fact, this is exactly the meaning of the first sentence of Art. 49 par. 3. It seems important that this sentence does not speak of attacks but of "sea warfare", which includes all acts committed in connection with belligerent interference with neutral or enemy shipping, *e. g.*, capture, seizure or destruction of vessels or goods at sea, or enforcing of a blockade against the enemy's coast and ports. However sea warfare includes naval bombardment of military objectives on land as well, since they may cause collateral damage.

The CDDH may have construed the language "sea warfare which may affect the civilian population ... on land" more restrictively. Otherwise it would have made no sense to add in the next sentence that the provisions "further apply" to all attacks from the sea. But even if one could overcome these difficulties by assuming that the last sentence of Art. 49 par. 3 is merely an obscurantistic tautology, the question remains why then the caveat "but do not otherwise affect the rules of international law applicable in armed conflict at sea" is attached to the rule concerning attacks and not to the broader stipulation dealing generally with all effects of sea warfare on the civilian population on land. In addition, a distinction between naval warfare which affects the civilian population on land and belligerent acts against the enemy's fleet would not suffice, because it is incompatible with Art. 49 par. 4. Since Part IV of Protocol I deals with the civilian population in general and not only with wounded, sick and shipwrecked civilians, the term "humanitarian protection" cannot be construed in a restrictive manner.

Another question is whether the scope of this provision is limited to the collateral damage at sea, in other words, to the incidental loss of civilian life, injury to civilians, damage to civilian objects, or a combination thereof, which would be disproportionate in relation to the military advantage anticipated from an attack against an enemy warship or aircraft at sea (*e. g.*, attacks against a submerged submarine with depth charges while shipwrecked civilians are drifting on rafts or swimming for their lives in these waters), or whether the protection of civilians and civilian objects at sea against the effects of hostilities has a broader meaning, including, *e. g.*, the rules of visit and search, the rules of destruction of enemy property at sea, *etc.* In the latter case, rules concerning the destruction of prizes at sea would come under the purvue of Art. 49 par. 4, which, for example, would tie in such humanitarian provisions as Art. 50 of the Declaration of London of 1909 providing that before a merchant vessel is destroyed all persons on board must be placed in safety,[216] and par. 2 of the London Naval Protocol of 1936 on submarine warfare, which stipulates that except in the case of persistent refusal to stop on being duly summoned, or of active resistance to visit and search, a warship may not sink or render incapable of navigating a merchant vessel without having first placed passengers and crew in a place of safety.[217] If that interpretation is correct, however, then what is left of the exception in the last sentence of Art. 49 par. 3 ?

It seems that these treaty provisions were drafted without sufficient knowledge of the specific and sometimes peculiar difficulties of the law of naval warfare. At sea, as opposed to land warfare, the distinction between combatants and non-combatants has a different connotation. To be sure, only warships are legally competent to exercise belligerent rights and in turn are subject to attack and destruction. The liability to attack and destruction is the consequence of the privileged combatant status, which is never enjoyed by a merchant vessel. Merchant ships by definition are civilian objects. Nonetheless, under the law of naval warfare, any merchant vessel, even under a neutral flag, could become a legitimate military objective liable to attack and destruction due to the performance of certain acts, such as blockade-running, refusal to stop, or resisting visit and search. Such civilian objects would then be treated like a combatant ship, without however being entitled to exercise belligerent rights like a man of war.

A viable interpretation of Art. 49 has to achieve the aim of making both the exception in the last sentence of par. 3 and par. 4 make sense

---

216 *Hinz/Rauch* (note 1), No. 1531; see also, *supra*, note 8.

217 *Hinz/Rauch* (note 1), No. 1532.

together. This can be done if one restricts the exception in par. 3 to the rules of naval warfare concerning operations against the enemy's fleet or aircraft and to attacks on naval forces at sea from land. This kind of interpretation seems to have been applied by a commission of legal experts of the German Red Cross who, in a Handbook on the Geneva Conventions and on the Additional Protocols, quote examples of international conventions coming under Art. 49 par. 4 and expressly mention the London Naval Protocol of 1936 on Submarine Warfare.[218]

Good faith interpretation, in accordance with the ordinary meaning to be given to the terms of Protocol I in their context and in the light of its object and purpose,[219] suggests the following construction of Art. 49 of Protocol I: The provisions of Section I of Part IV

— apply to all acts of naval warfare which may affect the civilian population, individual civilians or civilian objects on land, including attacks from the sea against military objectives on land and measures against the maritime commerce of the enemy whether under its own flag or under neutral flags;

— apply to all other acts of naval warfare as far as the effects of hostilities on civilians and civilian objects on land, at sea, or in the air are concerned, as regulated by conventional or customary international humanitarian law, including collateral damage of operations against enemy warships and effects of belligerent acts against merchant ships;

— do not affect other rules of naval warfare, including belligerent action against the enemy's fleet or other military objectives at sea or in the superjacent airspace and attacks from land against ships at sea or aircraft in the superjacent airspace.

This interpretation does not lead to a result which is manifestly absurd or unreasonable. In view of the effort necessary to bring into line the provisions of Art. 49 the opinion may indeed be justified that the meaning is still left sufficiently ambiguous so that recourse may be had to supplementary means of interpretation, notably the preparatory work of the CDDH.[220]

---

[218] Handbuch des Deutschen Roten Kreuzes zum IV. Genfer Rotkreuz-Abkommen und zu den Zusatzprotokollen, vol. 2, Bonn 1981, 158 note 2; see also, the reference to note 1 on page 156.

[219] Art. 31 Law of Treaties.

[220] Art. 32 Law of Treaties.

2. Preparatory Work

Draft Protocol I, submitted by the ICRC, contained in Art. 44 a provision on the field of application of the combat rules which reads as follows:

"1. The provisions contained in the present Section apply to any land, air or sea warfare which may affect the civilian population, individual civilians and civilian objects on land.

2. These provisions apply to acts of violence committed against the adversary, whether in defence or offence. Such acts are referred to hereafter as "attacks".

3. These provisions are complimentary to such other international rules relating to the protection of civilians and civilian objects against effects resulting from hostilities as may be binding upon the High Contracting Parties, in particular to Part II of the Fourth Convention."[221]

In the Commentary the ICRC explains that only military operations liable to cause effects on land are the object of this Section. As these operations would obviously be directed from the air or the sea as well as from points on land it was thought necessary to qualify them accordingly. As regards civilians at sea and in the air (in aircraft, balloons and other objects in flight) they were, according to the ICRC, not deprived of all protection since other norms of international law, principally customary law are applicable to them.[222]

With respect to par. 3 the Commentary states: "... The purpose of Art. 44 is not to revise but to supplement the existing law in force in particular the Fourth Convention ... The other norms of international law are essentially those of customary law, or are to be found in other conventions, such as the Hague Convention No. IV of 1907 and the Regulations annexed thereto, the Hague Convention No. IX of 1907 and the Hague Convention of 1954."[223]

Leaving aside the connotation of "supplementing" as opposed to "revising" it seems clear from the language in par. 1 and the examples given in par. 3 that the ICRC intended its draft to cover the effects of military operations at sea on land only. It is significant, therefore, that the CDDH did not accept this draft, but made several important changes.

During the first session of the CDDH it was a hotly debated issue, whether the words "on land" in Art. 44 par. 1 should be deleted. This

---

221 ICRC, Draft Additional Protocols to the Geneva Conventions of 12 August 1949, Commentary, Geneva 1973, 15.

222 *Op. cit.*, 54.

223 *Op. cit.*, 55.

deletion would have extended the applicability of Protocol I to all civilians and civilian objects on land, at sea or in the air. The delegates of naval powers insisted on the retention of the words "on land" in order to exclude the application of Protocol I to attacks on merchant ships which they asserted to be covered by other bodies of law such as the law of blockade and of visit and search.[224] The delegate of Great Britain pointed out that customary law for the protection of civilians and civilian ships in the case of warfare at sea differed greatly from that proposed in the draft Protocol. Under both bodies of law civilians included crews and passengers in merchant ships and non-combatant passengers in warships, although the protection granted to them must obviously differ from one category to the other. Merchant ships, some of which were armed in wartime, were entitled by customary law to use their arms in self-defense and were thus in a very different category from the civilian objects referred to in the draft Protocol. Under the London Protocol of 1936 a submarine or other warship was permitted in wartime to sink a merchant vessel, provided the passengers and crew were removed to a place of safety. In the case of refusal to stop or of resistance to visit and search, a warship was entitled to sink a merchant vessel without taking such precautions. There was thus a substantial contradiction between the customary and conventional law relating to merchant ships and the more comprehensive protection which it was proposed to grant to civilian objects under Protocol I. The rules of sea warfare perhaps needed to be codified or possibly changed, but a great deal of preparatory work would first be requested to resolve the contradictions he had mentioned.[225] The further statement made by the British delegate deserves to be emphazised that the qualified experts who had held lengthy discussions with a view to establishing a clear set of rules for the guidance of those who had to engage in warfare had not taken the existing law of sea warfare into account. Any attempt to make draft Protocol I apply to such warfare would weaken the efforts which had been made to give a clear lead in the field of humanitarian law.[226] The delegate of Belgium stressed that the rules of naval warfare were so specific that the provisions of draft Protocol I could not be applied to them.[227] The delegate of the Soviet Union expressed his satisfaction with the language of Art. 44 par. 1, but if the majority of the Committee wished the term "on land" to be defined, some explanations might be added at the end of the paragraph.[228]

---

[224] Official Records of the Diplomatic Conference on the Reaffirmation and Development of International Humanitarian Law applicable in Armed Conflicts, Bern 1978 (in the following abbreviated "O. R.") vol. XV, 236.

[225] *Op. cit.*, vol. XIV, 21.

[226] *Op. cit.*, 22.

[227] *Op. cit.*, 29.

The Working Group to which the article was referred, was unable to achieve a generally acceptable text for this paragraph and referred back to the III. Committee among others the question whether to delete the words "on land". By 35 votes to 33, with 4 abstentions, it was decided to retain them. When it was proposed to submit the entire paragraph to a vote, the Committee was unable to reach agreement on the place in which the words "on land" should be inserted in the paragraph. It was accordingly decided by 41 votes to 21 with 17 abstentions, to return the entire paragraph to the Working Group for further study.[229] The Working Group was unable to complete its consideration of the question at the first CDDH session.[230] It proved impossible to arrive at any convergence of views on the wording of Art. 44 par. 1. The Working Group was of the view that an important matter of substance about the territorial scope of application of the Section was involved and was unanimously of the view that Protocol I should "at least" cover military operations on land and military operations from the sea and air against persons and objects on land, notably in the form of bombardment, which affect civilians on land. Beyond that there was disagreement. Delegations were of differing views whether the Section should be applicable to operations at sea, *e. g.* blockade, sinking of merchant ships *etc.*, which affect civilians at sea, such as crews and passengers of ships, or on land. It was recognized that naval warfare is now regulated by various conventions and by a body of customary international law, but it was not clear to the Working Group how Protocol I might modify or affect this body of law. There was a widespread, but not unanimous, view in the Working Group that there could be no further progress on this paragraph until further study had been given to these questions.[231] It might be added that several delegations submitted amendments which would have clearly confined the scope of application of this Section to collateral effects on land, but they were not accepted.[232]

In the discussion of paragraph 3 of Art. 44 in the Working Group and in the Committee difficulties were also encountered with the word "complimentary", a word which was thought by some to lend a measure of ambiguity to the paragraph. Other delegations considered that the words "complètent" in French and "completan" in Spanish had a precise meaning and expressed correctly and in an appropriate manner that the

[228] *Op. cit.*, 30; see also, vol. XV, 237.

[229] *Op. cit.* vol. XV, 236, 237.

[230] *Op. cit.*, 272.

[231] *Op. cit.*, 255.

[232] *Op. cit.*, 257; Belgium and United Kingdom: "The provisions contained in the present section apply to attacks against the adversary on land which may affect the civilian population, individual civilians or civilian objects." Australia submitted an identical suggestion, see, Doc. CDDH/III/10 and 21 Corr. 1.

Protocol was intended to supplement the Conventions so that the latter would be applied in future as supplemented by the Protocol. The Working Group recommended the substitution of the words "in addition" for "complimentary". A number of delegations were in favor of provisions which did not jeopardize the protection provided by other treaties or by international customary law.[233] The text recommended by the Working Group was adopted by 73 votes to none, with 2 abstentions. The paragraph as adopted read: "The provisions of the present Section are in addition to the rules with respect to humanitarian protection contained in the Fourth Convention, particularly Part II thereof, and in such other international conventions as may be binding upon the High Contracting Parties, as well as to other rules of international law relating to the protection of civilians and civilian objects on land, at sea, or in the air, against the effects of hostilities."[234] It is noteworthy that the CDDH at this early stage already included the express reference to civilians and civilian objects at sea in this article.

In reviewing the discussion about the words "on land" one is somewhat flabbergasted as to how a provision even including these words could not directly affect the law of blockade or contraband. The words "on land" excluded the blockade measures at sea as such and the acts of contraband control at sea as such, however not their effects on the civilian population because they were felt on land. If it had been intended to exclude any repercussions on the law of blockade and contraband any reference to military operations at sea should have been deleted. A restriction on attacks from the sea against military objectives on land would, in this case, have been in order. The unfinished text after the first session of the CDDH read as follows: "The provisions contained in the present Section apply to any land, air or sea military operations against the adversary (on land) which may affect the civilian population, individual civilians or civilian objects (on land)."[235]

At the second session of the CDDH there was almost complete agreement in the Working Group that it would be both difficult and undesirable in the time available to try to review and revise the law applicable to an armed conflict at sea. It was also widely recognized that care should be taken not to change that body of law inadvertently through the provision, which later became Art. 49 par. 3. According to the Committee Report the solution was found through a combination of the ICRC text with a sentence which stated clearly that except for attacks against objectives on land, the law applicable to armed conflict at sea is

[233] O. R. (note 224), vol. XV, 237.

[234] *Op. cit.*, 238.

[235] *Op. cit.*, 236.

unaffected.[236] Several delegations remained dissatisfied with the draft recommended by the Working Group and subsequently adopted by the Committee. They objected to the phrase "on land" in the first sentence and to the second sentence as a whole. They preferred that this section of the Protocol should affect the law applicable to conduct of warfare at sea to the extent that the provisions of this Section would be more favourable to civilians than the existing law.[237] The text which was submitted to the Committee at its twenty-fourth meeting on 25 February 1975 read as follows: "The provisions contained in the present Section shall apply to any land, air or sea warfare which may affect the civilian population, individual civilians or civilian objects on land. They shall further apply to all attacks from the sea or the air against objectives on land, but do not otherwise affect the existing generally recognized rules of international law applicable to armed conflict at sea or in the air."[238]

The question whether to include the words "on land" and the part of the second sentence "but do not otherwise affect the rules of international law applicable in armed conflict at sea or the air" were submitted to a separate vote. The term "on land" was adopted by 56 votes to 1 with 7 abstentions and the portion of the second sentence referred to was adopted by 56 votes to 1 with 9 abstentions. The paragraph was then adopted by 60 votes to none, with 7 abstentions.[239]

As for Art. 44 par. 3 of the draft it remained unchanged during the second session.

And this was the end of any discussion on this issue at the CDDH. After two more sessions in 1976 and 1977 the plenary adopted this article by consensus without any representative taking the floor and no delegation considered it worthwhile to file a declaration or statement of understanding.[240] As *Waldemar Solf*, the legal expert of the United States delegation puts it, the issue had faded into oblivion.[241] In his Commentary *Solf* stresses that this paragraph reaffirms and clarifies existing protections and creates some new ones.[242]

If the second sentence of Art. 49 par. 3 could be construed as being a clarification or interpretation of the first sentence the provisions of

---

236 *Op. cit.*, 272.

237 *Ibid.*

238 *Op. cit.*, 302.

239 *Op. cit.*, 272; see also, vol. XIV, 218.

240 *Op. cit.* vol. VI, 208 at 19.

241 *Waldemar Solf*, in: *Michael Bothe/Karl-Josef Partsch/Waldemar Solf*, New Rules for Victims of Armed Conflicts, Commentary on the Two 1977 Protocols, The Hague 1982, 291.

242 *Ibid.*

Section I of Part IV of Protocol I would, indeed, be applicable only in cases of attacks by naval forces against military objectives on land. There are indications that at least the Working Group and Committee II were inclined to achieve this result. However, after the adoption of Protocol I this interpretation is not tenable, because it would be in direct contradiction to the treaty text. The second sentence of Art. 49 par. 3 is clear and unambiguous in so far as it commences with the words "They *further* apply" (Elles s'appliquent *en outre* / Se aplicarán *tambien* / Oni *takže* primenjajutsja) which has been correctly rendered into German by the translation conference convened by Austria, Switzerland and the Federal Republic of Germany as "Er (der Abschnitt) findet *ferner* Anwendung".[243] In the event that the second sentence had been meant to explain the foregoing provision words like "therefore", "consequently" *etc.* had to be used. To restrict Art. 49 par. 3 to attacks by naval forces against military objectives on land would be tantamount to a treaty interpretation *contra legem.* If one has to choose between the textual and teleological interpretation on the one hand and the supplementary means of interpretation on the other, the *travaux préparatoires* cannot prevail. The interpretation of the black letter text according to the general rule of interpretation as codified in the Vienna Convention on the Law of Treaties is the only acceptable solution.[244] The more so in our case since a restrictive interpretation *contra legem,* based upon preparatory work two years before the Protocol was adopted by the CDDH would be incompatible with Art. 49 par. 4 as illustrated by the reference to the London Naval Protocol of 1936 by the German Red Cross legal expert group.[245]

---

[243] *Hinz/Rauch* (note 1), No. 1575.

[244] Art. 31 Law of Treaties.

[245] See, *supra,* note 207.

V. Attacks from the Sea against Objectives on Land

1. Prohibitions and Restrictions

Without ignoring the differences which may exist in respect of bombardment between war on land and naval war, it cannot be denied that when bombardment is directed by naval forces against the land this operation is not a purely naval one. This already led the Third Committee of the Second Hague Peace Conference in 1907 to recommend the application of the fundamental principles ruling bombardment by land forces to bombardment of towns, villages and habitations by belligerent naval forces.[246] The basic principle of all warfare, that of distinction, which Protocol I endeavours to reinstate to its former position before it became buried under the rubble of target area bombardments and carpet bombings of cities, towns and villages in World War II like Coventry, Dresden and Hiroshima, was already contained in the Hague Convention No. IX of 1907 concerning Bombardment by Naval Forces in Time of War.[247]

This Convention, while forbidding the bombardment by naval forces of undefended ports, towns, villages, dwellings or buildings[248] expressly exempted from this prohibition military works, military or naval establishments, depots of arms or war material, workshops or plants which could be utilized for the needs of the hostile fleet or army, and ships in the harbor.[249] It further provided that in bombardments by naval forces all the necessary measures must be taken by the commander to spare as far as possible sacred edifices, buildings used for artistic, scientific, or charitable purposes, historic monuments, hospitals and places where the sick or wounded are collected on the understanding that they are not used at the time for military purposes.[250]

The same distinction between civilian objects and military objectives was the foundation of the 1954 Convention for the Protection of Cultural

[246] Report to the Conference, in: *Scott* (note 83) vol. I, 111.

[247] *Hinz/Rauch* (note 1), No. 1529.

[248] Art. 1.

[249] Art. 2.

[250] Art. 5.

Property in the Event of Armed Conflict.[251] This treaty is applicable to all naval bombardments. If there were any doubts, they should be removed by the final provisions according to which the Convention of 1954 is supplementary to Hague IX and shall substitute for the emblem described in Art. 5 of the Hague Convention of 1907 the emblem described in Art. 16 of the 1954 Convention.[252]

For the first time in the history of the law of war Protocol I actually merges completely the regulations of bombardment by naval forces and bombardment by land forces. The most important provisions of Protocol I shall be briefly summarized. There are nine important general provisions:

1. Only combatants and other military objectives may be proper targets for naval bombardment.[253] As far as objetcs are concerned military objectives are limited to those objects which by their nature, location, purpose or use make an effective contribution to military action and whose total or partial destruction, capture or neutralization, in the circumstances ruling at the time, offers a definite military advantage.[254] The civilian population as such as well as individual civilians or civilian objects shall not be made the object of bombardment by naval forces.[255] Acts or threats of violence by naval forces the primary purpose of which is to spread terror among the civilian population are prohibited.[256]

2. Naval bombardments of non-defended localities or demilitarized zones are strictly prohibited.[257]

3. Those who plan, decide upon or execute a naval bombardment have to pay attention to the rule of doubt. In case of doubt, whether a person is a civilian or whether an object which is normally dedicated to civilian purposes, is being used to make an effective contribution to military action, that person shall be considered to be a civilian and the object shall be presumed not to be so used.[258]

4. The naval commander has to identify the military objective on land properly. He has to do everything feasible to verify that the

---

251 The Convention was adopted on 14 May 1954, see, *Hinz/Rauch* (note 1), No. 1510.

252 Art. 36.

253 Art. 48.

254 Art. 52 par. 2.

255 Arts. 51 par. 2, 52 par. 1.

256 Art. 51 par. 2.

257 Arts. 59, 60.

258 Arts. 50 par. 1, 52 par. 3.

objectives to be bombarded are neither civilians nor civilian objects and are not subject to special protection but are military objectives.[259]

5. Indiscriminate naval bombardments are prohibited. Indiscriminate naval bombardments are

— those which are not directed at a specific military objective,

— those which employ a method or means of combat which cannot be directed at a specific military objective, or

— those which employ a method or means of combat the effects of which cannot be limited as required by Protocol I, and consequently, in each such case, are of a nature to strike military objectives on land and civilians or civilian objects without distinction.[260]

6. Naval area bombardment is prohibited, *i. e.* bombardments which treat as a single military objective a number of clearly separated and distinct military objectives located in a city, town, village or other area containing a similar concentration of civilians or civilian objetcs.[261]

7. Collateral damage, *i. e.* loss of civilian life, injury to civilians or damage to civilian objects incidental to naval bombardment against legitimate military objectives on land must not be excessive in relation to the concrete and direct military advantage anticipated.[262]

8. Care shall be taken in naval bombardment to protect the natural environment against widespread, long-term and severe damage. This protection includes a prohibition of the use of methods or means of naval bombardment which are intended or may be expected to cause widespread, long-term and severe damage to the natural environment.[263]

9. As precautionary measures those who plan or decide upon naval bombardment shall

— when a choice is possible between several military objectives on land for obtaining a similar military advantage, select that objective the bombardment of which may be expected to cause the least danger to civilian lives and to civilian objects;[264]

— take all feasible precautions in the choice of means and methods of bombardment with a view to avoiding and in any event to minimizing

---

[259] Art. 57 par. 2 (a) (i).

[260] Art. 51 par. 4.

[261] Art. 51 par. 5 (a).

[262] Art. 51 par. 5 (b).

[263] Arts. 35 par. 3, 55 par. 1; the ramifications of these provisions on naval warfare not related to the bombardment of military objectives on land are discussed *infra* in chapter XIII.

[264] Art. 57 par. 3.

incidental loss of civilian life, injury to civilians and damage to civilian objects;[265]

— give effective advance warning of a bombardment which may affect the civilian population, unless circumstances do not permit;[266]

— refrain from deciding to commence any naval bombardment which may be expected to cause excessive collateral damage;[267]

— cancel or suspend naval bombardments if it becomes apparent that the objective is not a military one or is subject to special protection or that the bombardment may be expected to cause excessive collateral damage.[268]

Of equal importance are three more specific Protocol provisions:

1. The naval bombardment of historic monuments, works of art or places of worship which constitute the cultural or spiritual heritage of peoples is prohibited.[269]

2. It is prohibited to bombard objects indispensable to the survival of the civilian population such as foodstuffs, agricultural areas, crops, livestock, drinking water installations and supplies and irrigation works for the specific purpose of denying them for their sustenance value to the civilian population or to the adverse Party. This prohibition does not apply to such objects which are used as sustenance solely for the members of the enemy armed forces or in direct support of military action, provided, however, that such bombardment must not leave the civilian population with such inadequate food or water as to cause its starvation or to cause it to move away.[270]

3. Works or installations containing dangerous forces, namely dams, dykes and nuclear electrical generating stations shall not be made the object of naval bombardment, even where these objects are military objectives, if such naval bombardment may cause the release of dangerous forces and consequent severe losses among the civilian population. This prohibition includes military objectives located at or in the vicinity of these works or installations if such bombardment may have the results indicated above. The protection, however, ceases, if dams, dykes or nuclear power stations or other military objects mentioned above contribute or are used in regular, significant and direct support of

---

[265] Art. 57 par. 2 (a) (ii).

[266] Art. 57 par. 2 (c).

[267] Art. 57 par. 2 (a) (iii).

[268] Art. 57 par. 2 (b).

[269] Art. 53. This norm is without prejudice to the provisions of the Hague Convention of 14 May 1954 (note 251).

[270] Art. 54.

military operations and bombardment is the only feasible way to terminate such support.[271]

These complex and sometimes vague, obscure or ambiguous provisions of Protocol I create a whole crop of extremely difficult problems of interpretation for the conduct of war on land and for air warfare against the background of such modern concepts as Air-Land-Battle, Follow-On Forces Attack or Second Echelon Interdiction in densely populated areas. They are the direct result of the tactical move by the ICRC, not to submit to the CDDH specific prohibitions of certain weapons or methods of combat which may be deemed to be excessively injurious or to have indiscriminate effects, but to establish a complex interwoven system of restraints, restrictions, prohibitions and demands for precautionary measures.[272] These difficulties may well be exacerbated for naval bombardment in a future armed conflict by the dramatic changes in the technology of combat in the marine environment, for instance the use of submarine-launched cruise missiles and other over-the-horizon weapons.[273] It would transgress the scope of this paper to analyze in detail these interpretative problems or the possible effect of the statements of understanding made at the CDDH or on the occasion of the signing of Protocol I.[274] For our purposes it might suffice to state in general that whatever legal interpretations of these rules for air warfare and war on land are deemed viable and compatible with object and purpose of Protocol I have to be applied to naval bombardment against military objectives on land as well. However, the critical issue whether the above mentioned rules on weapon restraint apply to conventional naval bombardments only or do regulate also naval bombardment with nuclear warheads, shall be singled out and dealt with in the next subchapter.

2. Use of Nuclear Weapons

Whether the combat provisions of Protocol I apply to nuclear weapons or not is highly important in an era of strategic submarines, carrying intercontinental ballistic missiles tipped with multiple independently

---

[271] Art. 56.

[272] *Elmar Rauch,* Attack Restraints, Target Limitations and Prohibitions or Restrictions of Use of Certain Conventional Weapons, in: RDPMDG vol. XVIII-1-2 (1979), 51—72; see also in this context, *Elmar Rauch,* Le concept de nécessité militaire dans le droit de la guerre, in: RDPMDG vol. XIX-1-2 (1980), 218—237.

[273] See, *Alex L. Parks,* Submarine-launched Cruise Missile and International Law: A Response, in: US Naval Institute Proceedings, September 1977, 120 *et seq.*; *Daniell Patrick O'Connell,* The Legality of Naval Cruise Missiles, in: AJIL vol. 66 (1972), 785—794 (785 *et seq.*).

[274] See, *Elmar Rauch,* The Protection of the Civilian Population in International Armed Conflicts and the Use of Landmines, in: GYIL vol. 24 (1981), 262—287.

targetable warheads or equipped with long-range nuclear-capable cruise missiles, both weapon systems being able to deliver devastating strikes at the adversary's territory thus constituting an important part of nuclear deterrence. Submarine-launched ballistic missiles (SLBM) are indispensable for deterrence, notably assured second strike capability of the superpowers. The sea-based element of the nuclear triad forms part of an effective system of mutual deterrence.

Protocol I does not expressly refer to nuclear weapons or conventional weapons, but deals in Part III generally with methods and means of warfare and in Part IV Section I with the general protection of the civilian population against effects of hostilities. The treaty text is clear, unambiguous and intelligible for everyone, be he lawyer or layman, soldier or civilian. The relevant provisions apply to "any land, air or sea warfare" and to "all attacks" from the sea or air against objectives on land.[275] In order to ensure respect for and protection of the civilian population and civilian objects, the parties to the conflict must "at all times" distinguish between the civilian population and combatants and between civilian objects and military objectives.[276] And the provisions prohibiting indiscriminate attacks[277] and protecting the natural environment[278] refer to any "method or means of warfare". This simplicity and clarity of the wording in the combat provisions of Protocol I cannot simply be disregarded. There is nothing, absolutely nothing in the text of Protocol I that states or implies that the prescriptions and prohibitions formulated in this treaty do not apply to a certain category of weapons. Hence it follows, that Protocol I does apply also to all attacks from the sea against objectives on land with nuclear warheads. This result is in accordance with the decisions of the Permanent Court of International Justice and of the International Court of Justice on treaty interpretation[279] and with the rules of the 1969 Vienna Convention on the Law of Treaties.[280] Customary international law as evidenced by court judgments as well as the Vienna Convention does not permit an interpretation of the Protocol I provisions other than in a manner compatible with their terms. Or, to phrase it differently, a treaty provision must be interpreted in accordance with the ordinary meaning to be given to its terms. And neither context nor *travaux préparatoires,* if recourse may be had to the latter at all, can justify an interpretation which would

[275] Art. 49 par. 3.

[276] Art. 48.

[277] Art. 51 paras. 4, 5.

[278] Art. 35 par. 3, Art. 55.

[279] PCIJ (1925) Series B, No. 11, 39; PCIJ (1927) Series A, No. 10, 16; PCIJ (1932) Series A/B, 377, 378; ICJ, Recueil, 1950, 8; ICJ, Recueil, 1960, 159, 160.

[280] Art. 31, 32.

lead, in fact, to manifestly absurd and unreasonable results. The exclusion of nuclear weapons from the scope of application of Protocol I would do exactly that. The military commander facing a situation where only an attack violating new rules of Protocol I would prevent a decisive advance of the enemy could lawfully achieve precisely that result by ordering that conventional grenades be exchanged for nuclear warheads. A forbidden target for conventional weapons would become a legitimate military objective for nuclear weapons, a monstruous contradiction to the object and purpose of Protocol I. It does not come as a surprise, therefore, that most scholarly writings on the subject reach the conclusion that the provisions of Protocol I do apply to the use of nuclear weapons.[281] It should be added that such an interpretation of "humanitarian" law would result in lowering the nuclear threshold and thus run counter to the efforts to raise the nuclear threshold while maintaining a credible deterrence, symbolized by catchwords like Second Echelon Interdiction, Air-Land-Battle 2000, Follow-On-Forces-Attack or Deep Strike, all new concepts within the framework of NATO's strategy of flexible response.

Opposing views have been expressed by two members of the United States CDDH delegation. Their writings reflect the official position of the US at the Conference.[282] Beyond that there is one scholar whom I consider to be the most eminent and best known of the French experts on the contemporary law of war who tries to prove that Protocol I does not regulate the use of nuclear weapons. Founded in the highest ethical motives this scholar wants to convince his government that it should sign and ratify Protocol I.[283] His arguments, however, do not stand up to closer scrutiny.

---

[281] *Knut Ipsen*, in: *Michael Bothe/Knut Ipsen/Karl-Josef Partsch*, Die Genfer Konferenz über humanitäres Völkerrecht, in: ZaöRV vol. 38 (1978), 1—85 (43, 44); *Stanislaw E. Nahlik*, Droit dit "de Genève" et droit dit "de la Haye": unité ou dualité?, in: AFDI vol. 24 (1978), 9—27 (26); *Bernhard Graefrath*, Zum Anwendungsbereich der Ergänzungsprotokolle zu den Genfer Abkommen vom 12. August 1949, in: Staat und Recht, vol. 29 (1978), 133—146; *Elmar Rauch*, L'emploi d'armes nucléaires et la réaffirmation et le développement du droit international humanitaire applicable dans les conflits armés, in: Revue Hellénique du Droit International vol. 33 (1980), 53—110; see also, *Claude Pilloud*, Les Conventions de Genève de 1949 pour la protection des victimes de la guerre, les Protocoles additionnels de 1977 et les armes nucléaires, in: GYIL vol. 21 (1978), 169—179; *Pilloud*, ICRC director, couches his opinion in diplomatic terms, "without wishing to take a stand on either side of the question" (*op. cit.* 177). However, *Pilloud* wrote the memorandum of the ICRC dated 28 October 1980 (see, *infra*, note 289) according to which Protocol I is applicable to nuclear weapons. See also, *Allan Rosas*, International Law and the Use of Nuclear Weapons, in: Essays in Honour of *Erik Castrén*, Helsinki 1979, 73—95.

[282] *George H. Aldrich*, New Life for the Laws of War, in: AJIL vol. 75 (1981), 764—783 (780, 781); unfortunately this article creates more difficulties and poses more questions than it is designed to solve; *Solf*, in: *Bothe/Partsch/Solf* (note 241), 188—192.

While the theory of those who exclude nuclear weapons from Protocol I rests primarily on a "consensus" theory, there are more and more disturbing sidelines to the effect that deterrence with nuclear weapons in peacetime may be lawful, while the use of nuclear weapons in armed conflict might not.[284] If a democracy would try to threaten an aggressor with a weapon that it cannot use under international law, a potential adversary would no longer be deterred, because such an adversary knows how powerfully constrained a democracy is by public opinion. Open societies must not ignore the rules of international law in the pursuit of strategic objectives, including the preservation of a global balance of deterrence. The West cannot change its responsiveness to the rule of law and would never do so even if it could.

The device to exclude nuclear weapons from the scope of application of Protocol I is an alleged "consensus" as contextual agreement, which has to be read into the text of Protocol I. In other words, the black letter text of this treaty instrument is incomplete and misleading. It can be understood only together with such a corrective contextual agreement, which together with Protocol I forms an *ensemble normatif.*[285] For want of space I may be permitted to restrict myself to some brief remarks on that theory.[286] It starts with the preparatory work of the ICRC and ends with the statements of understanding of the United States and the United Kingdom on the occasion of the signing of Protocol I. The ICRC in its introduction of the 1973 draft Protocols stated: "Problems relating to atomic, bacteriological and chemical warfare are subjects of international agreements or negotiations by governments, and in submitting these

---

[283] *Henri Meyrowitz,* La stratégie nucléaire et le Protocole additionnel I aux Conventions de Genève de 1949, in: RGDIP vol. 83 (1979), 905—961; *idem,* Le statut des armes nucléaires en droit international — le partie, in: GYIL vol. 25 (1982), 219—251.

[284] *Meyrowitz,* GYIL vol. 25 (note 283), 223: "Aucune des raisons qui obligent le moraliste et le juriste à reconnaître la licéité (ou la non-illicéité) de la dissuasion dans l'ordre de la paix n'est valable dans l'ordre de la guerre et ne permit de transposer cette licéité dans le droit de la guerre. A cette intransmissibilité de la licéité de la dissuasion à l'emploi des armes atomiques correspond l'intransmissibilité à la dissuasion de la réglementation de cet emploi par le *ius in bello.* Ce qui est permis dans l'ordre de la dissuasion ne l'est pas dans celui de l'emploi; ce qui est interdit dans delui-ci ne l'est pas dans celui-là." And at 224: "Ce mème droit international qui reconnaît, dans l'ordre de la paix, la légalité de la dissuasion, réglemente, dans l'ordre de la guerre, l'emploi des armes nucléaires, d'une façon très restrictive, interdisant pratiquement dans la grande majorité, voire dans la quasi-totalité des cas l'exécution des menaces nucléaries stratégiques les plus significantes."

[285] *Meyrowitz,* GYIL vol. 25 (note 283), 236: "... quant à la question de l'applicabilité du traité aux armes nucléaires, il faut compléter, c'est-à-dire corriger, la lecture du texte de l'instrument par le contenue du consensus", and at 237: "... il faut tenir compte, à côté du texte de cet instrument, du consensus sur les armes nucléaires, lequel forme avec le Protocole un ensemble normatif."

[286] For a detailed discussion, see, *Rauch* (note 281).

draft Protocols the ICRC does not intend to broach these problems."[287] Whatever such a statement may be worth for the treaty adopted in 1977, one has to take into consideration at least that the same ICRC stated in the Commentary to the draft, which appeared four months later: "It should be recalled that, apart from some provisions of a general nature, the ICRC has not included in its draft any rules governing atomic, bacteriological and chemical weapons."[288] And all the important combat provisions of Protocol I, from the protection of the natural environment to the principle of distinction and identification and the prohibition of indiscriminate attacks are of a "general nature". By the way, after the adoption of Protocol I the Legal Department of the ICRC issued a memorandum which avoids the issue of strategic nuclear weapons, but declares in unmistakable terms that the use of so-called miniaturized nuclear warheads is regulated by Protocol I.[289] This proves beyond any doubt that the ICRC did not intend at all to exclude nuclear weapons from the scope of application of the general combat provisions of Protocol I. Attention should be paid also to the fact, that the ICRC treats nuclear, chemical and biological weapons the same way. The American legal expert, who wrote the first commentary on the Protocol I combat provisions repeats the official US position that nuclear weapons are excluded but at the same time in the context of Art. 55 admits that the protection of the natural environment against widespread, long-term and severe damage affects such "unconventional means of warfare as the massive use of herbicides or chemical agents "which could produce such damage.[290]

The ICRC statements of 1973 have two consequences. First, they prove that the ICRC made no distinction between conventional and unconventional (nuclear, chemical and biological) weapons. There would be no prohibition as to any particular category of weapon, be it conventional or nuclear, or to any use of certain specific types of weapons. Second, it was self-evident for the ICRC that the general provisions of Protocol I would apply to all weapons, including nuclear, chemical and biological weapons, and in particular their effects on the civilian population.

---

287 ICRC, Draft Additional Protocols to the Geneva Conventions of 12 August 1949, Geneva 1973, 2.

288 ICRC Commentary (note 221), 2.

289 ICRC, Division Juridique, Doc. COM/KUR/13 *bis* of 28 October 1980, 12: "Il existerait depuis quelques annés des projectiles nucléaires 'miniaturisées' dont les effets pourraient être limités aux objectifs militaires contre lesquels ils seraient employés. Si donc un belligérant prenait la décision, grave de conséquences, d'employer de tels projectiles, il devrait, au moins, respecter les restrictions prévues par le Protocole."

290 *Solf*, in: *Bothe/Partsch/Solf* (note 241), 188—191 and 348.

During the CDDH the US, UK and French delegations made statements of understanding according to which their governments were of the opinion that Protocol I was not intended to regulate the use of nuclear weapons.[291] The French government decided not to sign Protocol I because it could accept neither the provisions of Art. 51 (4) and 57 (2) regarding indiscriminate attacks, nor the provisions of Art. 52 pertaining to the general protection of civilian objects, nor those of Art. 58 (b) recommending that the Parties to a conflict avoid locating military objectives within or near densely populated areas; apart from the most explicit reservations on the ambiguity of Articles 51, 52, 57 and 58.[292] This leaves us with the statements of understandings of the two Anglo-Saxon powers, who repeated their position at the signing of Protocol I as follows. The government of the United States signed subject to the condition that "it is the understanding of the United States of America that the rules established by this Protocol were not intended to have any effect on and do not regulate or prohibit the use of nuclear weapons".[293] The government of Great Britain for its part declared that it was signing the Protocol on the basis of certain conditions, including the understanding "that the new rules introduced by the Protocol are not intended to have any effect on and do not regulate or prohibit the use of nuclear weapons".[294]

The whole "consensus"-theory is based on the assumption that all the other more than 100 CDDH delegations were in agreement with this exemption and that by silence a material consensus was reached which has to be read into the text of the otherwise misleading Protocol I. This contextual agreement is described as half-explicit and half-implicit, as unwritten and tacit, implied and unusual and it is, furthermore, suggested that the delegates who allegedly took part in this consensus did not even know what they were doing, because they were not aware of its content and implications.[295] It is mere fiction that there is a coexistence of the Protocol text and of an unwritten accord.[296]

---

291 Actes de la Conférence diplomatique sur la réaffirmation et le développement du droit international humanitaire, applicable dans les conflits armés, Genève (1974—1977), Berne 1978 (in the following abbreviated 'Actes'), vol. V, 129, 136 par. 36; vol. XIV, 466 par. 123; vol. VII, 199 par. 3; 301 par. 82; 310 par. 119.

292 Actes (note 291) vol. VII, 200 par. 3.

293 Declarations made at time of signature, annexed to the notification of the Swiss Federal Political Department of 16 January 1978 (411.619.0), at 2, reproduced in AJIL vol. 72 (1978), 407.

294 *Op. cit.*, at 4.

295 *Meyrowitz*, RGDIP vol. 83 (note 283), 909, 916, 917, 920, 927, 928, 932, 938, 942, 952; see, *Rauch* (note 281), 74—76.

296 *Meyrowitz*, GYIL vol. 25 (note 283) at 229: "Cette originalité, la coexistence du texte du Protocole et d'un accord non écrit, accompagnant cet instrument et

First of all, all those delegations who wanted the Protocol to expressly prohibit any use of nuclear weapons and were unsuccessful in obtaining such an express treaty provision, can be safely assumed to be in favor of the application of the general provisions of Protocol I to the use of nuclear weapons, since such a result is at least a step in the direction of their suggestions. In other words, it is a violation of the *animus contrahendi* of all delegations who tabled such proposals to pretend that they took part in a "consensus" to the contrary. This includes Albania, China, Ghana, Peoples Republic of Korea, Iraq, Philippines, Romania and Yugoslavia.[297] In accordance with Art. 31 of the Vienna Convention on the Law of Treaties, the context includes any agreement relating to the treaty which was made between "all the parties" in connection with the conclusion of the treaty.[298] And it was not only the above mentioned delegations who never thought about taking part in such contextual agreement. Those who are familiar with the conditions, under which scholars and scientists have to work in Eastern Europe, will have no doubt, that the articles published by *Stanislaw Nahlik* and *Bernhard Graefrath* on this sensitive issue would not have seen the light if they were not compatible with the official position of Poland and the GDR.[299] It seems, therefore, almost superfluous to draw attention to the declaration of India in its explanation of its vote on Art. 35. The Indian delegation expressly stated that the new rule on the protection of the natural environment against widespread, long-term and severe damage to the natural environment would apply to all categories of weapons, to wit, nuclear, bacteriological, chemical or conventional, or any other category of weapon.[300] When the Swiss government, on 18 February 1981 submitted Protocol I to the Swiss Parliament for ratification it, too, stated unambiguously that the new rule on the protection of the natural environment as well as all rules of customary international law and conventional international law of war as amended by Protocol I are applicable to the use of nuclear weapons.[301] More as a footnote, it may be

---

ayant trait à son contenu, diffère à ce point du droit commun des traités qu'il incombe à celui qui l'affirme de rapporter la preuve du consensus sur les armes nucléaires ..."

[297] Actes (note 291) vol. XIV, 76 par. 87; vol. V, 116 par. 18; see also, vol. XVI, 27 par. 6; vol. V, 92 par. 36; vol. XIV, 260 par. 31; vol. V, 119 par. 32; vol. IX, 274 par. 23; vol. V, 99 par. 36 and vol. XVI, 30 par. 16; see also, vol. V, 82 par. 31, 100 par. 20.

[298] Art. 31 par. 2 (a).

[299] See, *supra*, note 281.

[300] Actes (note 291) vol. VI, 114.

[301] Botschaft des Schweizerischen Bundesrates über die Zusatzprotokolle zu den Genfer Abkommen of 18 February 1981, 20, 21: "Protokoll I ... dürfte kaum geeignet sein, praktisch oder rechtlich die von Nuklearkriegen aufgeworfenen Probleme zu lösen. Keine Bestimmung bezieht sich ausdrücklich auf den Einsatz

added, that there was even no consensus between the three western nuclear powers. According to the French position Protocol I covers only the case of an armed conflict waged with conventional weapons. That means its provisions become totally inapplicable from the moment in an armed conflict when a belligerent resorts to atomic weapons.[302] In contrast, both the US and the British statements consider that in such a case the Protocol remains applicable and binding upon the Parties, and that only the use of nuclear weapons as such is not regulated by this treaty instrument. However, the statements of understanding of the two Anglo-Saxon powers are incompatible with each other in a different aspect. Whilst the US statements excludes the "rules established by Protocol I", the British statement refers to the "new rules introduced by the Protocol".[303] Finally I may mention that also the ICRC in the above mentioned memorandum of 28 October 1980 flatly rejects the "consensus" theory out of hand.[304]

The proponents of the contextual "consensus", of course, have to qualify the nuclear statements of understanding as unnecessary but useful.[305] Since they only repeat a "consensus" they can never be a reservation and therefore, do not have to meet the compatibility test with object and purpose of Protocol I.[306] This goes even beyond what the legal expert on the US CDDH delegation considers tenable. The above mentioned Commentary on Protocol I follows the official US position that it would be inconsistent with the understanding, expressed in the relevant statements of the US and of Great Britain, to denominate these

---

von Atomwaffen; dieser ist expressis verbis weder verboten noch eingeschränkt. Dennoch darf man davon ausgehen, daß einige allgemeine Vorschriften des Protokolls, insbesondere soweit sie auf die Haager Landkriegsordnung zurückgehen, auch für die Kernwaffen gelten: die allgemeine Beschränkung des Rechts der Konfliktparteien in der Wahl der Methoden und Mittel der Kriegführung (Art. 35 Abs 1), die Pflicht der Konfliktparteien, zwischen der Zivilbevölkerung und Kombattanten sowie zwischen Zivilobjekten und militärischen Zielen zu unterscheiden und Operationen streng auf militärische Ziele zu beschränken (Art. 48 und 51 Abs. 4 und 5), das Verbot, Methoden oder Mittel zur Kriegführung zu verwenden, die ausgedehnte, langanhaltende und schwere Schäden der natürlichen Umwelt verursachen (Art. 35 Abs. 3 und 55) sowie das Verbot, Waffen, Geschosse oder Material sowie Methoden der Kriegführung zu verwenden, die unnötige Leiden verursachen (Art. 35 Abs. 2). Man kann also dafürhalten, daß der Einsatz von Kernwaffen den Beschränkungen des Völkergewohnheitsrechts und des vertraglichen Völkerrechts, wie es durch das Protokoll ergänzt ist *(sic!)*, unterliegt."

[302] *Meyrowitz* tries to smooth over these important discrepancies by declaring them *formules imprudentes*, GYIL vol. 25 (note 283), 238.

[303] For details, see, *Rauch* (note 281), 86—88.

[304] See, ICRC Doc. (note 289), 8: "Il ne peut s'agir d'un consensus au sens juridique actuel du terme."

[305] *Meyrowitz*, RGDIP vol. 83 (note 283), 939, and GYIL vol. 25 (note 283), 240.

[306] Art. 19 (c) Vienna Convention on the Law of Treaties.

declarations as reservations. The author adds, however, that any state which disagrees with this interpretation, may treat such declarations as reservations.[307]

There was only one material consensus reached at the CDDH: the text of Protocol I. No unwritten, tacit, implied, half-implicit, half explicit, unusual contextual consensus exists whereby the interpreter is bound to presume a massive derogation from the unambiguous wording of the treaty provisions. The proponents of a nuclear "consensus" as contextual agreement which has to be read into Protocol I simply fail to make a credible case. Their high ethical motivation, to contribute to a wide ratification of Protocol I including all nuclear powers, misleads them to tamper with basic rules of treaty interpretation. Their position is tantamount to the equation: nuclear weapons are no "normal" weapons, consequently Protocol I does not have to measure up to "juridical normality".[308] The idea of a contextual nuclear "consensus" which contradicts the clear and unambiguous language of the agreement actually reached, and which sacrifices the very object and purpose of Protocol I is preposterous. And to invoke the abnormality of nuclear weapons in order to violate the *animus negotiandi* and the *animus contrahendi* of more than 100 delegations at a codification conference and to do away with customary and conventional rules of treaty interpretation is very naive indeed.

---

[307] *Solf* (note 282), 191 footnote 12.

[308] *Meyrowitz*, GYIL vol. 25 (note 283), 236: "Les armes nucléaires ne sont pas un sujet "normal", auquel puissent s'appliquer les standards de la normalité juridique." Interestingly enough, for the proof of the "consensus" *Meyrowitz* refers in the first place to common sense (see, 229). What would have been more reasonable than for instance replace the heading of Part III Section I "Methods and means of Warfare" by "Conventional Methods and Means of Warfare" if this was what the CDDH intended to say.

VI. Imposition of a Blockade

The law of belligerent measures and sanctions against the sea-borne commerce of the enemy or neutral States is commonly referred to as the law of prize. In order to evaluate any changes brought about by Protocol I in this body of law it is indispensable to identify and state the pertinent rules of prize law as they stood before 1977. To be sure, it is beyond the scope of this analysis to attempt to obtain a comprehensive view of the status of the totality of the rules constituting this branch of international law. But even if brief outlines only are envisaged, there is ground for hesitation, because the institutions of the traditional law of prize seem to have been melted down to mere elements of the concept of "economic warfare" at sea or even withered away. The terms of reference of the Ministry of Economic Warfare set up in Great Britain at the beginning of World War II defined this term as follows: "Economic warfare is a military operation comparable to the operations of the three Services in that its object is to defeat the enemy, and complementary to them in that its function is to deprive the enemy of the material means of resistance. But, unlike the operations of the armed forces, its results are secured not only by direct attack upon the enemy but also by bringing pressure to bear upon those neutral countries from which the enemy draws his supplies. It must be distinguished from coercive measures appropriate for adoption in peace to settle international differences without recourse to war, *e. g.* sanctions, pacific blockades, economic reprisals *etc.* since, unlike such measures, it has as its ultimate sanction the use of belligerent rights."[309] It is quite obvious that such a definition is not compatible at all with any distinction between military needs and civilian needs and, consequently, does not square with the object and purpose of a treaty which endeavours to reinstate and considerably develop this distinction. By the same token, this kind of warfare is not apt to favor clearcut distinctions between different instruments of naval warfare which, in both World Wars, have been disregarded to an extend that even contraband control and blockade could no longer be separated. Nevertheless, for clarity's sake some basic structures have to be presupposed in order to judge the impact of Protocol I.

[309] *W. N. Medlicott,* The Economic Blockade, vol. I, London 1952, 172; see also, *Karl Zemanek,* article "Economic Warfare", in: *Bernhardt* (note 25), 158—163.

1. Legal Regime

In order to avoid lengthy discussions of many a controversy of the law of naval blockade, the following observations are based mainly on the most recent editions of the Manuals of Naval Warfare of the two nations left who have a blue water navy, the United States of America and the Union of Soviet Socialist Republics. In addition, reference is made to the teaching of the most highly qualified publicists within the meaning of the Statute of the International Court of Justice.[310] It is submitted, furthermore, that the Declaration of Paris concerning the regulation of maritime warfare, signed 16 April 1856[311] is still in force and legally binding those States who are parties to it. This declaration is the most important convention on our subject concluded during the past century. However, it consisted only of four operative clauses on privateering, contraband and blockade. The Declaration of London concerning the Law of Maritime War, adopted by the London Naval Conference on 26 February 1909,[312] basing itself on the Declaration of Paris, drafted a much more comprehensive treaty, consisting of 71 articles, which, in my opinion, corresponded and correspond in substance with the generally recognized principles of international law as expressly stated by the signatories.[313] Even if the Declaration of London was never adopted in legally binding form, it is legitimate to make reference to its articles in order to identify the rules of prize law, since it was largely a restatement of pre-existing customary law applicable to the operation of warships.

A blockade is a belligerent operation intended to prevent vessels of all States from entering or leaving specified coastal areas which are under the sovereignty, under the occupation or under the control of an enemy. Such areas may include ports and harbors, the entire coastline or parts of it. A blockade may be declared either by the government of the blockading State or by the commander of the blockading force acting on behalf of his government. A blockade, in order to be binding, must be effective. This means that a blockade must be maintained by

---

[310] BGBl 1973 II, 430, 505; as far as German authors are concerned, there is only one worth to be mentioned, *Ferdinand Paul Perels*, who dealt in two volumes with all relevant problems: Das allgemeine öffentliche Seerecht im Deutschen Reiche, Berlin 1901, and: Das internationale öffentliche Seerecht der Gegenwart, 2nd ed., Berlin 1903.

[311] See, *supra*, note 6.

[312] See, *supra*, note 8.

[313] Preliminary provision before Chapter I, which reads as follows: "The signatory Powers are agreed that the rules contained in the following chapters correspond in substance with the generally recognized principles of international law."

a force sufficient to render ingress and egress to or from the blockaded area dangerous. A blockade must not bar access to or departure from neutral ports or coasts. A blockade must be applied impartially to the vessels and aircraft of all States. It is customary for the blockade to be notified in a suitable manner to the government of all States because knowledge of the existence of a blockade is essential to the offences of breach of blockade and attempted breach of blockade. Vessels and aircraft are liable to capture for breach of blockade and attempted breach of blockade. The liability of a blockade runner to capture begins and terminates with her voyage or flight. If a vessel or aircraft has succeeded in escaping from a blockaded area, liability to capture continues until the completion of the voyage or flight.[314]

Notwithstanding hotly disputed details of the law of naval blockade, there has never been any doubt that blockade as such is a legitimate belligerent act. In view of the reaffirmation and development of the law of war in Protocol I a brief look at the law of warfare on land might be helpful particularly since the Final Act of the Second Hague Peace Conference stipulates expressly: "The Conference records the wish that the preparation of regulations relative to the laws and customs of naval war should figure in the programme of the next conference, and that, in any case the powers should apply as far as possible, to war by sea, the principles of the Convention relative to the Laws and Customs of War on Land."[315] A naval blockade can be compared to a land siege, the difference being that a siege aims at the capture of the besieged place, whilst a blockade endeavours merely to interrupt all sea-borne commercial intercourse of the enemy. As for a land siege "no rule of law exists which obliges a besieging force to allow all non-combatants, or even women, children, the aged, the sick and wounded or subjects of neutral Powers, to leave the besieged locality unmolested. Further, should the commander of a besieged place expel the non-combatants, in order to lessen the number of those who consume his store of provisions, the besieging force need not allow them to pass through its lines, but

[314] Declaration of Paris (note 6), par. 4; Declaration of London (note 8), Art. 1—21; US LNW (note 54), No. 632; USSR NILM (note 54), 440—445; it should be noted that according to the Soviet Manual of Naval Warfare effectiveness is not regarded as necessary for the legality of a blockade (*op. cit.*, 441); *Perels*, Seerecht der Gegenwart (note 310), 261—279; *Constantine John Colombos*, A Treatise on the Law of Prize, 3rd ed., London 1949, 253—283; *idem*, The International Law of the Sea, 4th ed., London 1961, 649—677; *Ludwig Weber*, article "Blockade", in: *Bernhardt* (note 25), 47—51; *Lassa Francis Lawrence Oppenheim/Hersch Lauterpacht*, International Law, vol. 2, 7th ed., London 1952, 796—800; *Robert W. Tucker*, The Law of War and Neutrality at Sea, Washington 1957, 283—317.

[315] British Parliamentary Papers, Miscellaneous No. 6 (1908), Command Paper 4175, 15.

may drive them back."[316] Similarly, the Field Manual of the United States Army states that, save for exceptions provided for in international conventions, there is no rule of international law which compels the commander of an investing force to permit non-combatants to leave a besieged locality. "Thus, if a commander of a besieged place expels the non-combatants in order to lessen the logistical burden he has to bear, it is lawful, though an extreme measure, to drive them back, so as to hasten the surrender."[317]

2. State Practice

Here again, a reservation seems in order. It is impossible within the framework of this paper, to give a complete account of the experiences in World Wars I and II. Therefore, I might be excused to focus attention on some features of naval warfare which are of paramount importance for the analysis of Protocol I which will be undertaken in the following chapter. And there is a second point which should be underscored right at the outset in order to avoid misunderstandings. The interplay of the operation of reprisals is intentionally disregarded here. Chapter XIII *infra* will be devoted entirely to this aspect of State practice.[318]

a) World War I

Upon the outbreak of hostilities, at the beginning of August 1914, the government of the United States urged all nations concerned, whether belligerent or neutral, to adopt the Declaration of London as a temporary code of naval warfare. The Central Powers replied that they would abide by the Declaration provided their enemies observed it too. The British government replied on 22 August 1914 that it had decided "to adopt generally the rules subject to certain modifications and additions which

[316] *Oppenheim/Lauterpacht* (note 314), 419.

[317] The Law of Land Warfare (note 210), No. 44; see also, Kriegsrechtliche Einzelschriften, herausgegeben vom Großen Generalstabe, Heft 31, Kriegsbrauch im Landkriege, Berlin 1902, 20, 21 which reads as follows: "Will der Kommandant einer Festung die Verteidigungsfähigkeit seines Platzes dadurch erhöhen, daß er einen Teil der Bevölkerung (Frauen, Kinder, Greise, Kranke, Verwundete etc.) ausweist, so hat er diese Maßregel rechtzeitig, d. h. vor dem Eintreten der Einschließung erfolgen zu lassen. Ist diese letztere vollzogen, kann ein Recht auf freien Abzug dieser Elemente nicht geltend gemacht werden; alle dahin zielenden Forderungen von Lehrern des Völkerrechts sind im Prinzip als mit den Grundsätzen des Krieges im Widerspruch stehend mit Entschiedenheit zurückzuweisen. Gerade das Verbleiben dieser Personen kann die Übergabe des Platzes unter Umständen wesentlich beschleunigen; es wäre daher eine Torheit des Belagerers, auf diesen Vorteil freiwillig zu verzichten."

[318] See, *infra*, Chapter XIII, 154—162.

they judge indispensable to the efficient conduct of their naval operations." The French and Italian governments followed suit with similar reservations. This was deemed unacceptable to the American government particularly in view of Art. 65 of the Declaration of London[319] and in a telegram of 22 October 1914 the US Secretary of State withdrew the suggestion.[320]

The deviations from the stipulations of the Declaration of London enacted by the Entente Powers were manifold. They all were considered "rendered necessary by the special conditions of the present war".[321] In other words, the rules and regulations of the law of naval warfare were subjected to the principle of military necessity. Even if one could agree on the Declaration of London as a yardstick it is difficult to qualify the Allied measures against the sea-borne commerce of the Central Powers. The term "blockade" was never mentioned in any of the pertinent British Orders in Council or the corresponding French Decrees.[322] However, the new law of contraband[323] applied by the Entente Powers amounted to a blockade without meeting the requirements set forth by the generally recognized rules of naval warfare at that time. Despite the language in all legal and administrative acts, which carefully avoided the term "blockade", this term was actually used since the very beginning of the war in diplomatic exchanges and parliamentary debates. Gradually this word came to be employed as a comprehensive description of the whole system under which the maritime commerce of the Central Powers was destroyed.[324] The Entente governments had ordered the seizure, detention or destruction of all goods of German origin, ownership or destination and the capture and condemnation or destruction of all vessels carrying goods of enemy origin or destination encountered at sea on their way to or from a port in any neutral country affording means of access to the enemy territory without calling at an Allied port.[325] Interestingly, the competent British authority for all measures of economic warfare against the Central Powers, was called "Ministry of Blockade".[326]

---

[319] Art. 65 reads: "The provisions of the present Declaration must be treated as a whole, and cannot be separated."

[320] *James Wilford Garner*, International Law and the World War, London 1920, vol. I, 31, 32.

[321] *Colombos*, Law of Prize (note 314), 26.

[322] *Colombos*, Law of the Sea (note 314), 267.

[323] See, *infra*, 95—101.

[324] See, *e. g.*, Correspondence between His Majesty's Government and the United States Government respecting the rights of belligerents, Parliamentary Papers, Miscellaneous No. 6 (1915), Command Paper 7816, 26; *Malkin* (note 12), 87.

[325] *Colombos*, Law of Prize (note 314), 266, 267.

[326] *Medlicott* (note 309), 1.

This blockade by the Entente Powers was not only not effective within the meaning of the Declaration of Paris or the Declaration of London, it was also not restricted to the ports and coasts belonging to or occupied by the enemy, but barred access to neutral ports and coasts. Nor was it applied impartially, because the German Baltic ports were left open to traffic with Denmark, Norway and Sweden. Finally, the Entente Powers altered the rule which forbids the application of continuous voyage in respect to blockade so as to authorize the capture of vessels bound to non-blockaded ports.[327] Another arbitrary expedient adopted by the Entente for extending the blockade to neutral ports was the system of "rationing" neutrals, which included foodstuffs. The Entente based itself on statistics which showed the amount of customary imports for domestic needs before the war of all neutrals that had land or short sea communications with Germany. Where such neutral countries were found to be importing greater quantities of goods on the contraband list it was presumed that the surplus ultimately found its way to Germany and these goods were seized, placed in prize and eventually condemned. Neutral States protested vigorously against this infringements upon their rights to trade with each other, which was a blatant violation of international law.[328]

Other devices to strangle neutral trade were the so-called "Skinner scheme", "White-ship" agreements and the British policy to refuse bunker coal at British ports to neutral merchant vessels whose owners refused to comply with certain regulations designed to prevent cargoes from going to the Central Powers. Under the scheme suggested by *Mr. Skinner*, the American Consul General at London, the British embassy at Washington upon application of American exporters investigated the consignments and cabled the facts to the Contraband Committee in London. If the consignment was permitted to pass the blockade a "Letter of assurance" was issued. "White-ship" agreements were concluded between the British government and neutral shipping lines whose vessels were exempted from the blockade upon their undertaking to transfer to the British authorities for adjudication by the prize courts any goods which were suspected of being destined for enemy countries. The vessels entitled to this privileged treatment were known as "white ships".[329] All these measures set the stage for the development of the so-called Navicert-system. The term is an abbreviation for "navigation certificate". American traders started in March 1916 to avail themselves of "navicerts" which were patterned after the "Letters of

[327] *Colombos*, Law of Prize (note 314), 266—277; *Garner* (note 320) vol. II, 319—339.

[328] *Garner* (note 320) vol. II, 344—347.

[329] *Op. cit.*, 344—349.

assurance" and were tantamount to a commercial passport for unimpeded passage through the British blockade to a neutral destination.[330]

As to the legal qualification of these measures of the Entente Powers they raised a considerable controversy regarding the problem which set of rules should be applied, blockade[331] or contraband control.[332] In avoiding the term "blockade" the Entente Powers, obviously, thought to be better equipped to exploit the *clausula rebus sic stantibus* argument. There could not be the slightest doubt that all accepted principles of international law concerning blockade were violated, but at the same time the Entente Powers maintained as a point of law that the rules of "close blockade" were changed by the normative power of facts (or military necessity) to a different type of blockade which for want of a better term was called "long distance blockade". It is breathtaking to see that the legal community in the Entente countries had no difficulties at all to understand and justify these violations of customary and conventional international law of naval warfare with the modern conditions, range of shore batteries and torpedo boats, action of submarines and mines *etc.*,[333] while at the same time similar considerations and actions with respect to submarine warfare undertaken by the Central Powers were unequivocally condemned as barbaric crimes.[334]

The measures of the Entente Powers were denounced by the United States of America (before it joined the war) and other neutral countries as being contrary to the law of blockade and, therefore, without justification. The American government in a diplomatic note described the measures as a "so-called blockade" which was "illegal in conception and nature".[335]

The Central Powers and sympathizing neutral countries attacked the long-distance blockade as a "starvation blockade". The German chancellor in a speech on 15 April 1916 declared it to be in violation of international law because it seeks "to starve us out and to extend the war to the entire German nation, to our women and our children".[336] In 1919 the German government stated that more than half a million deaths in Germany had resulted from malnutrition or undernutrition due to the

[330] *H. Ritchie*, The "Navicert" System during the World War, Washington 1938, 1 *et seq.*

[331] So, *e. g.*, *Malkin* (note 12), 87—98; *Colombos*, Law of Prize (note 314), 267.

[332] So, *e. g.*, *Erle Richards*, The British Prize Courts and the War, in: BYIL vol. 1 (1920—21), 11—34; *J. A. Hall*, The Law of Naval Warfare, 2nd ed., London 1921, 195.

[333] *Colombos*, Law of Prize (note 314), 268, 269.

[334] See, *infra*, Chapter VIII.

[335] *Garner* (note 320) vol. II, 321.

[336] *Op. cit.*, 336.

Entente starvation blockade between the autumn of 1916 and the end of the year 1918. The German delegation at the Versailles Peace Conference submitted a claim for compensation on account of the suffering and deaths caused by the blockade. In his address at the opening session on 7 May 1919, the head of the German delegation, *Count Brockdorff-Rantzau,* stated that "hundreds of thousands of non-combatants who have perished since 11 November 1918 by reason of the blockade were killed with cold deliberation after our adversaries had conquered and victory had been assured them".[337] Needless to say the Conference did not even answer the charge.

b) World War II

Due to the attitude of the victorious powers of World War I to only consider rules regulating submarine warfare as subject for international codification conferences[338] the chaotic state of the law of naval blockade had not changed at all by the outbreak of World War II. The process of "adopting" generally recognized rules of international law to "new circumstances", *i. e.* to considerations of military necessities of the Allied Powers continued. As the name "Ministry of Economic Warfare" for the successor of the British "Ministry of Blockade" shows, the efforts to destroy the whole sea-borne commerce of the enemy were even more far-reaching, more comprehensive and more sophisticated than in World War I.

In addition to the interception of ships at sea as blockade runners, their diversion into port, the examination and eventual condemnation of their cargo, two techniques were of paramount importance, which had developed during the previous war, rationing and navicerting. All legal difficulties inherent in the condemnation of goods under the "rationing system" simply on statistical grounds were overcome by the prize courts of the Allied Powers, mostly by throwing the burden of proof that the cargo was not going ultimately to the Axis Powers upon the owner of the goods.[339]

The other main technique was the so-called navicert system, this time used on a much more considerable scale. The method was extended in July 1940 by the British government to all sea-borne cargoes shipped to every neutral European port and to the Spanish and international zones of Morocco and the Spanish and Portuguese Atlantic islands. All vessels sailing from a neutral port to any such destination were required

337 *Ibid.*

338 See, *supra*, 12—13.

339 For details, see, *Gerald G. Fitzmaurice,* Some Aspects of Modern Contraband Control and the Law of Prize, in: BYIL vol. 22 (1945), 85—95.

to obtain "cargo-navicerts" for every item of their consignment and in addition a "ship-navicert" at the last port of loading. The British Order in Council of 31 July 1940 formally declared that all goods not covered by a "cargo navicert" would be liable to seizure. And all ships sailing to Europe without a "ship navicert" would be treated as blockade runners liable to seizure in prize. To supplement this system, Great Britain introduced, in August 1940, a pass called a "ship's warrant" issued to vessels whose owners or charterers had in contractual form agreed that their ships would not carry contraband. In 1942 the "navicert" system was linked to the "ship's warrant" method, in that no navicerts were issued to ships which did not possess a ship's warrant.[340]

A number of neutral governments lodged protests against this compulsory navicert system which they attacked as a gross violation of the law of nations. They even prohibited their citizens to submit to any investigation before competent foreign authorities. The German Supreme Prize Tribunal held, that the acceptance of a navicert constituted an act of unneutral service.[341]

In the final analysis all these measures of the Allied Powers during World War II, again, constituted a "longdistance blockade" which extended to neutral ports and coasts. The British Order in Council of 21 July 1940 was only consequential in declaring all neutral ships, which refused to comply with the compulsory navicert system "blockade runners". In scholarly writings and government exchanges of notes the term "blockade" came up fairly soon.[342] *W. N. Medlicott* entitled his comprehensive review of the economic warfare against the Axis Powers between 1939 and 1945 "The Economic Blockade".[343]

In a *note verbale* of 17 September 1939 to the French government the German government accused Britain of "having formally introduced a starvation blockade against women and children".[344] In the British newspaper *Daily Herald* on 15 November 1939 an article protesting the British measures against the sea-borne commerce with Germany appeared under the headline "It's War on Babies".[345] Prime Minister *Chamberlain* made a statement on the British blockade in the House of Commons on 26 September 1939 in which he said: "Much play is made

[340] *Ibid.*

[341] *Dietrich Steinicke,* Das Navicertsystem, Hamburg 1966; *Colombos,* Law of Prize (note 314), 216—219; *Rolf Stödter,* Article "Safe-Conduct and Safe Passage", in: *Bernhardt* (note 25) vol. 4, 193—196; *Fitzmaurice* (note 339), 83—89.

[342] See, *e. g., Colombos,* Law of Prize (note 314), 281—283.

[343] *Supra,* note 309; see in particular, vol. I, chapters II and XIII "The Machinery of the Blockade", 63—132 and 430—467.

[344] Urkunden zum Seekriegsrecht (note 70), No. 2.

[345] *Medlicott* (note 309) vol. I, 46.

in German propaganda of the inclusion of foodstuffs in the category of conditional contraband and it is represented that we are thereby conducting an illegal and inhuman blockade. But in this respect a naval blockade is in no way different from a land siege and no one has ever suggested that a besieging commander should allow free rations to a besieged town."[346] The German *Charge d'Affairs* in a letter to the Norwegian shipowner *Halvorsen* wrote on 21 February 1940: "The German armed forces conduct the naval operations as a fight against the British blockade, which has as its goal the starvation of the German people. The more brutal and inhumane England tries to enforce this blockade, the tougher the defensive actions against it get ..."[347]

The British cabinet decisions of 25 June 1940 authorizing the application of the blockade measures to all parts of continental France and of 13 July 1940 extending them to all ships bound for French Morocco, Algeria and Tunisia, led to a heated discussion between London and Washington about relaxation of the blockade and allowing relief actions on behalf of the starving civilian population. On 5 July 1940 *Lord Lothian* warned the Foreign Office that there were indications that appeals to the humanitarian instincts of the American people must be anticipated. The Foreign Office answered with a formal statement of 15 July 1940, which argued that supplies admitted to occupied territories would either fall into enemy hands or release other supplies for the enemy and that it would be false humanity to lengthen the war by allowing the enemy to be assisted in this way.[348] In the American presidential election campaign *Mr. Hoover* seized upon the subject and said on 11 August 1940: "Somebody must raise a voice for food supply during the coming winter to the 27 million innocent civilians mostly women and children, in Norway, Holland, Belgium and Poland. Possibly France will also be in difficulties ... The obvious truth is there will be wholesale starvation, death and disease in these little countries unless something is done about it ... These little nations are being ground between the millstones of the food blockade. Great Britain and Germany against each other. They are blockaded by Germany from continental supplies and Great Britain from overseas supplies. The Germans blame the British blockade. The British say the fault is the German invasion."[349] Prime Minister *Winston Churchill* answered with the following statement on 20 August 1940: "There have been many proposals founded in the highest motives that food should be allowed to pass the blockade for the

[346] Parliamentary Debates, House of Commons, Fifth Series, vol. 351, 1237; Urkunden zum Seekriegsrecht (note 70), No. 28.

[347] Urkunden zum Seekriegsrecht (note 70), No. 4.

[348] *Medlicott* (note 309) vol. I, 449, 551.

[349] *Op. cit.*, 553, 554.

relief of these populations. I regret that we must refuse these requests. Many of these valuable foods are essential to the manufacture of vital war materials. Fats are used to make explosives. Potatoes make the alcohol for motor spirit. The plastic materials now so largely used in the construction of aircraft are made of milk. If the German use these commodities to help them to bomb our women and children rather than to feed the populations who produce them, we may be sure imported foods would go the same way, directly or indirectly, or be employed to relieve the enemy of the responsibilities he has so wantonly assumed."[350]

3. Protocol I

In this context there are two provisions of Protocol I which have to be scrutinized, Art. 70 and 54.

a) Relief Actions

Art. 70 par. 1 deals with relief in favour of the civilian population in the following way. If the civilian population of any territory under the control of a party to the conflict, other than occupied territory, is not adequately provided with food, medical supplies, clothing, bedding, means of shelter or other supplies, essential to the survival of the civilian population, relief actions which are humanitarian and impartial in character and conducted without any adverse distinction shall be undertaken subject to the agreement of the parties concerned. Offers of such relief shall not be regarded as interference in armed conflict or as unfriendly acts. This treaty obligation, obviously, is addressed to the whole community of nations, at least to all contracting parties. As far as the parties to the conflict are concerned, Protocol I specifies that they shall allow and facilitate rapid and unimpeded passage of all relief consignments, equipment and personnel, even if such assistance is destined for the civilian population of the adverse party.[351] They shall

---

[350] *Op. cit.*, 666.

[351] Art. 70 par. 2. This article is a development of the rules contained in Art. 23 of Geneva Convention IV of 1949, under which the contracting parties shall permit the free passage of all consignments of essential food-stuffs, clothing and tonics, intended for children under fifteen, expectant mothers and maternity cases. This obligation, however, is subject to the condition that the power, which permits its passage is satisfied, that there are no serious reasons to fearing, among others, that a definite advantage may accrue to the military efforts or economy of the enemy through the substitution of the above mentioned consignments for goods which would otherwise be provided or produced by the enemy or through the release of such material, services or facilities as would otherwise be required for the production of such goods. In addition, the power which allows the passage of the consignments may make such permission conditional on the distribution being made under the local supervision of the pro-

in no way whatsoever, divert relief consignments from the purpose for which they are intended nor delay their forwarding, except in cases of urgent necessity in the interest of the civilian population concerned.[352] Furthermore, the parties to the conflict shall protect relief consignments and facilitate their rapid distribution,[353] encourage and facilitate effective international coordination of the relief actions[354] and respect and protect personnel participating in relief actions.[355] There are, of course, safeguards. The parties to the conflict and the transit states have the right to prescribe the technical arrangements including search, under which rapid and unimpeded passage of relief consignments is permitted,[356] and may make such permission conditional upon the distribution of this assistance being made under the local supervision of a protective power.[357]

At first glance this looks like the end of any naval blockade. However, all relief actions shall be taken "subject to the agreement" of the belligerents, the transit state and the relief state. In the case of a naval blockade, does this mean in fact that the blockading party has to agree, in other words cannot refuse its consent? Or is it up to the discretion of the blockading power to reject any relief offers because of imperative considerations of military necessity or any other reason? It has been argued that both elements, the obligation to undertake relief actions and the requirement of an agreement have to have their weight, and that the agreement has to be granted as a matter of principle, but that it can be refused for valid and compelling reasons, which may include considerations of military necessity.[358] According to this theory there is no "unfettered discretion" to refuse agreement and it may not be declined for "arbitrary or capricious reasons" and a refusal to grant transit through a naval blockade with the intent to deprive the enemy population of food would not be based on a valid reason and amount to a violation of Art. 70 of Protocol I.[359]

This interpretation does not hold up to closer scrutiny. The CDDH did apply here a common drafting technique, that is to formulate a rule which gives the impression of an ironclad obligation, and at the same

---

tecting powers. However, the appointment of protecting powers is dependant upon the consent of the belligerents (Art. 9).

352 Art. 70 par. 3 (c).

353 Art. 70 par. 4.

354 Art. 70 par. 5.

355 Art. 71 par. 2.

356 Art. 70 par. 3 (a).

357 Art. 70 par. 3 (b); as for the protecting powers, see, Art. 5 Protocol I.

358 *Bothe*, in: Bothe/Partsch/Solf (note 241), 434.

359 *Op. cit.*, 434.

time took the bite out of that rule. A similar example is Art. 5 of Protocol I concerning the appointment of protecting powers. If the parties to a conflict can not consent to a protecting power they "shall accept without delay an offer ... by the ICRC or by any other organisation ... to act as a substitute". This, again, gives the impression that there is an automatic substitution in case of disagreement between the belligerents. Not so, because the provision continues: "The function of such a substitute is subject to the consent of the parties to the conflict."[360] This treaty-making technique has been applied by UNCLOS III as well. Under Art. 298 par. 1 LOS Convention a State may make an optional exception from the obligatory third party dispute settlement system with respect to delimitation disputes, provided he submits to conciliation, the results of which are not binding upon the parties.

If they cannot reach an agreement on the basis of the recommendation of the conciliation commission the parties shall "by mutual consent" submit the question to one of the compulsory procedures entailing binding decisions. Here as in Art. 70 Protocol I it is left to the discretion of the parties concerned to agree to a certain procedure or measure. For a different interpretation one should at least expect to see the language used *e. g.* in Art. 125 LOS Convention, dealing with transit of land-locked States to and from the sea. Par. 1 provides that land-locked States "shall enjoy freedom of transit" through the territory of the transit State. The terms and modalities, however, "for exercising freedom of transit" shall according to par. 2 be "agreed between" the land-locked State and the transit State concerned. Whatever this kind of transit right is worth, at least the land-locked State has a right of transit as such, whilst in the case of Art. 70 Protocol I we do not have a right of transit through a naval blockade for relief purposes with only the exercise of that right being subject to an agreement. The right of transit is dependent upon the consent of the other States concerned and the blockading power, consequently, has an unrestricted discretion to agree or not to the passage of relief consignments.

It is correct that in Art. 70 par. 2 the obligation to grant the agreement is clearer and more specific than in par. 1. Maybe, one could even share the view that par. 2 is *lex specialis* with respect to Art. 70 par. 1.[361] But par. 2 refers to relief provided "in accordance with this Section" thus incorporating also par. 1 which prevails over par. 2.

---

360 Art. 5 par. 4.

361 *Bothe* (note 358), 434.

b) *Starvation of Civilians*

Art. 54 par. 1 of Protocol I unambiguously provides that starvation of civilians as a method of warfare is prohibited. As a matter of consequence, naval blockades of the kind enforced by the Entente Powers and the Allied Powers in World Wars I and II and briefly described above would be in violation of Protocol I. Any blockade of the ports and coasts of an enemy, whose civilian population is not adequately provided with food would be a breach of the new law of armed conflict. The arguments put forth by Prime Minister *Churchill* in the British Parliament would be no longer tenable.[362]

This provision, based upon an amendment by Great Britain and Belgium[363] was accepted after considerable discussion in the Working Group of Committee III as a useful statement of a basic principle and as an important addition to the law protecting civilians. According to the Committee report the scope of the principle will be defined *inter alia* by the other relevant articles in the Protocol, particularly those dealing with relief actions.[364] From a dogmatic point of view this raises the question whether Art. 70 has to be interpreted in the light of Art. 54. In my view, faced with the specific language of Art. 70, analyzed above, Art. 54 has to be considered as the *sedes materiae*.

I do not hesitate to mention that the Australian delegation placed on the record of the CDDH its view that nothing in Art. 54 directly or indirectly affects existing legal rules concerning naval blockade.[365] And to give the whole picture (and underline again the difficulties of interpreting Protocol I) an observation from the Committee report should be quoted: "The fact that the paragraph does not change the law of naval blockade is made clear by Art. 44 par. 1."[366] This statement of the *rapporteur* is wrong, at least after the CDDH adopted the language that the provisions of Section I of Part IV apply to any sea warfare "which may affect the civilian population on land".[367] Even *Waldemar Solf*, who seems to be very restrictive in the interpretation of Art. 49 par. 3 as far as the law of naval warfare is concerned admits that the statement in the Committee report is wrong, carefully choosing his words, though, that Art. 54 par. 1 "indirectly ... may have had some effect on that law (of naval warfare)".[368]

---

362 See, *supra*, 89—90.

363 O. R. (note 224) vol. III, 218; see also, O. R. vol. XIV, 139.

364 *Op. cit.* vol. XV, 289.

365 *Op. cit.* vol. VI, 220.

366 *Op. cit.* vol. XV, 279 at 73.

367 See, *supra*, 57—66.

In my opinion it is beyond doubt that under Art. 54 par. 1 of Protocol I a naval blockade to prevent the import of foodstuffs in order to hasten the end of an armed conflict through starvation of the civilian population will be unlawful and a violation of Protocol I.

---

[368] *Solf*, in: *Bothe/Partsch/Solf* (note 241), 338; *sedes materiae* for him are the provisions dealing with relief actions in Arts. 70 and 71; see in particular, footnote 10 on 338; see also, 290, footnote 10.

VII. Control of Contraband

Again it seems appropriate to begin with a note of caution. What has been said with respect to the law of blockade applies *mutatis mutandis* to the law of contraband.[369]

1. Legal Regime

Contraband consists of all goods which are destined for an enemy and which may be susceptible to use in war. Contraband goods are divided into two categories, absolute and conditional contraband. Absolute contraband are goods whose very character makes them destined to be used in war or which are used primarily for war. Under the Declaration of London as absolute contraband may be treated arms and ammunitions of all kinds, projectiles, charges and cartridges, powder, explosives *etc.* Conditional contraband consists of goods which are equally susceptible to use either for peaceful or for warlike purposes. Upon the outbreak of armed conflict, the parties to the conflict may declare contraband lists, setting forth therein the classification of articles to be regarded absolute contraband or conditional contraband. Goods consisting of absolute contraband are liable to capture if their destination is the territory belonging to or occupied by an enemy. Goods consisting of conditional contraband are liable to capture if destined for the use of an enemy government or its armed forces. Vessels and aircraft carrying goods liable to capture as absolute or conditional contraband may be captured. However, liability to capture for carriage of contraband ceases once a vessel or aircraft has deposited the contraband goods.[370]

It is well to note that the London Declaration allows all foodstuffs to be treated as conditional contraband only.[371] This practice had prevailed for centuries. But with notable exceptions. France in its war against China in 1885 declared rice as absolute contraband when destined to

[399] See, *supra*, 80—82.

[370] Declaration of Paris (note 6) par. 2 and 3; Declaration of London (note 8), Art. 22—44; US LNW (note 54), NWIP 10-2, No. 631; USSR NILM (note 54), 446—448; *Perels* (note 314), 234—260; *Colombos* (note 321), 186—230; *idem* (note 322), 610—634; *Werner Meng*, Article "Contraband", in: *Bernhardt* (note 25) vol. 3, 122—125; *Oppenheim/Lauterpacht* (note 314), 801—805; *Tucker* (note 314), 263—282.

[371] Art. 24.

Chinese ports of Canton. Interestingly, the British government protested against this announcement with the following statement: "The British government could not admit that provisions would be treated as contraband of war merely because they were assigned to a belligerent port... Foodstuffs with a hostile destination can be considered contraband of war only if they are supplies for the enemy's forces. It is not sufficient that they are capable of being so used; it must be shown that this was in fact their destination at the time of seizure."[372] *Bismarck,* in reply to a memorandum from a couple of Hamburg merchants took a different point of view of the French announcement: "Any disadvantage our commercial and carrying interests may suffer by the treatment of rice as contraband of war does not justify our opposing the measure which it has been thought fit to take in carrying on a foreign war ... The measure in question has for its object the shortening of the war by increasing the difficulties of the enemy and is a justifiable step in war if impartially enforced against all neutral ships."[373]

In this context it should not be forgotten that there were already a century ago scholars and teachers of international law who were adamantly opposed to the law of prize in general and against the seizure of foodstuffs in particular which they considered barbaric and immoral.[374]

2. State Practice

a) World War I

By a succession of Ordinances and Decrees the Entente Powers put on the list of conditional contraband various articles which were on the free list in the Declaration of London of 1909 and put on the list of absolute contraband other articles which were on the list of conditional contraband in the Declaration. Although foodstuffs had from the outset been regarded as conditional contraband they were as early as 1915 in effect treated as absolute contraband.[375] Thus, when the American government protested against the unprecedented extension by the Entente Powers of the doctrine of contraband to goods formerly regarded

[372] *Garner* (note 320) vol. II, 291.

[373] *Op. cit.*, 337.

[374] See, *e. g., Johann Caspar Bluntschli,* Das Beuterecht im Krieg und das Seebeuterecht insbesondere, Nördlingen 1878, Nachdruck Amsterdam 1970, 79 *et seq.; idem,* Das moderne Völkerrecht der civilisierten Staaten als Rechtsbuch dargestellt, 3rd. ed., Nördlingen 1878, § 807; *Massé,* Le droit commercial dans ses rapports avec le droit de gens, Paris 1874, 186; *Perels* (note 314), 245 rejects these arguments as follows: "... So liegt hierin mindestens eine Verkennung des Wesens der Kriegsverhältnisse. Jeder Befehlshaber hat nicht nur das Recht, sondern auch die Pflicht, die Zufuhr von Lebensmitteln an den Gegner zu verhindern."

[375] *Garner* (note 320) vol. II, 285.

as innocent, the British Foreign Secretary in a diplomatic note of 10 February 1915 expressed the opinion that "the reason for drawing a distinction between foodstuffs intended for the civil population and those for the armed forces or enemy government disappears when the distinction between the civil population and the armed forces itself disappears. In any country in which there exists such a tremendous organization for war as now obtains in Germany, there is no clear division between those for whom the government is responsible for feeding and those whom it is not. Experience shows that the power to requisition will be used to the fullest extent in order to make sure that the wants of the military are supplied, and however much goods may be imported for civil use, it is by the military that they will be consumed if military exigencies require it, especially now that the German government has taken control of all the foodstuffs in the country."[376] A revealing statement in particular in the context of object and purpose of Protocol I.

By a proclamation of 19 April 1916 the British government formally abandoned the distinction between absolute and conditional contraband. The British Foreign Office explained the action with the following statement: "The circumstances of the present war are so peculiar that His Majesty's government consider that for practical purposes the distinction between the two classes of contraband has ceased to have any value. So large a proportion of the inhabitants of the enemy country are taking part, directly or indirectly, in the war that no real distinction can now be drawn between the armed forces and the civilian population. Similarly, the enemy government has taken control, by a series of decrees and orders of practically all the articles of the list of conditional contraband, so that they are now available for government use. So long as these exceptional conditions continue our belligerent rights with respect to the two kinds of contraband are the same and our treatment of them must be identical."[377] The foundation for total war at sea seems to have been layed not only by the submarine warfare of the Central Powers.

However, the Entente Powers not only abandoned the distinction between civilian needs and military needs by disregarding the traditional rules concerning absolute and conditional contraband. They also promulgated ordinances which extended the doctrine of continuous voyage or ultimate destination to the carriage of conditional contraband contrary to the Declaration of London.[378] These legislative acts stipulated

[376] Quoted by *Sir Samuel Evans* in *The Kim* (1915), see, *James Wilford Garner*, Prize Law During the World War, New York 1927, 554.

[377] *Garner* (note 320) vol. II, 287.

[378] Art. 35.

that vessels bound for neutral ports, if the goods were consigned "to order" or if they showed a consignee in enemy or occupied territory should be liable to capture.[379] In deviation from the Declaration of London the burden of proving an innocent destination was under all circumstances placed on the owner of the goods.[380] In October 1915 the governments of the Entente Powers announced that the rule "the neutral or enemy character of a vessel is determined by the flag which she is entitled to fly"[381] should no longer be regarded as in force. The particular reason for abrogating the article of the Declaration of London was to enable British and French prize courts to condemn certain merchant vessels flying the American flag, but in the ownership of which German citizens held a preponderating interest.[382]

Finally, the Entente Powers formally abrogated the Declaration of London completely. The British Order in Council of 7 July 1916, withdrawing the Declaration, nonetheless pretended that His Majesty's government was resolved "to exercise their belligerent rights at sea in strict accordance with the law of nations" — the usual attempt of all belligerents to cover up even outright and blatant violations of international law of war in legal garb. In a note addressed to neutral governments the British government justified its action by arguing that the generally accepted rules of international law could no longer be adhered to because "the mannifold developments of naval and military science, the invention of new engines of war, the concentration by the Germanic Powers of the whole body of their resources on military ends produced conditions altogether different from those prevailing in previous naval wars".[383] To phrase it a little bit more bluntly, the Entente Powers in order not to hamper their military efforts by a distinction between civilian objects and military objectives, civilian needs and military needs arrogated themselves the right to waive the rules and considered the law of naval warfare as a set of rules of convenience at their mercy. There is not the slightest doubt about the above mentioned mannifold developments,[384] but this line of argument could not be convincing when at the same time the attempts of the Central Powers to apply the same yardstick to the use of the submarine torpedo boat were qualified as war crimes.

---

[379] *Garner* (note 320) vol. I, 31, 32.

[380] *Op. cit.*, 31.

[381] Art. 57 Declaration of London.

[382] *Garner* (note 320) vol. I, 32.

[383] *Op. cit.*, 33.

[384] See, *supra*, 12—14.

b) *World War II*

The contraband lists issued at the outbreak of the Second World War did preserve the distinction between absolute and conditional contraband, food and foodstuffs being treated as conditional contraband.[385] However, this distinction from the very beginning proved more specious than real, and British prize courts held early in World War II that foodstuffs albeit only conditional contraband, were condemnable as good and lawful prize as a result of "the German decrees which imposed government control on these articles and prescribed that they were automatically seized at the moment of coming into the customs house". In *The Sidi Ifni* the British Privy Council affirmed the traditional rule that conditional contraband can only be condemned if it is proven that it will assist the warlike operations of the enemy, but added: "Under the existing circumstances all foodstuffs of necessity fall into this category."[386] For all objects and purposes there never existed in practice any distinction between the traditional categories of absolute and conditional contraband during World War II.

3. Protocol I

Purpose and destination have always been the distinguishing criteria of contraband. Articles exclusively used for war are also in the future subject to seizure and condemnation as prize. Insofar, Protocol I did not change the traditional basis of the law of naval warfare. With respect to dual use items or articles "susceptible of use in war as well as for purposes of peace"[387] this might be different. Art. 54 par. 2 of Protocol I prohibits the attack, destruction or removal or rendering useless of objects indispensable to the survival of the civilian population for the specific purpose of denying them for their sustenance value to the civilian population or to the adverse party, whatever the motive, whether in order to starve out civilians, to cause them to move away, or for any other motive. This provision covers all indispensable objects. The list — foodstuffs, agricultural areas for the production of foodstuffs, crops, livestock, drinking water installations and supplies and irrigation works — is illustrative and not exhaustive. Although it deals primarily with food and drinking water objects which contribute to their production, the open-ended character indicates that other life-sustaining objects such as clothing, shelter and fuel (coal,

[385] See the contraband lists of Great Britain, France, Germany and Italy as well as the diplomatic protests of neutral governments against them, in: Urkunden zum Seekriegsrecht (note 70), No. 39—72.

[386] *Colombos*, Law of Prize (note 314), 214, 215.

[387] Art. 24 Declaration of London.

heating oil, wood) may also be covered depending upon the geographical region and the climate conditions. It may be mentioned that *e. g.* Ghana tabled an amendment to insert "means of communication" in the list.[388] And 13 Arab States proposed the inclusion of "fuel reservoirs and refineries".[389]

A little confusion might be caused by the interplay of purpose and motive. The only action that is prohibited is that which is done for the purpose of denying the objects to the adverse party or to the civilian population. In principle that is fairly clear, but the sentence does not read easily, because that statement is followed by the words "whatever the motive that produced that purpose, whether to starve out civilians, to cause them to move away, or any other motive". There seems to be some surplus here, but the Working Group of Committee III was unable to come to an agreement on how to simplify it.[390]

The prohibition in Art. 54 par. 1 does not apply to such indispensable objects as are used by an adverse party as sustenance solely for the members of its armed forces or, if not as sustenance then in direct support of military activities, provided, however, that in no event shall action against these objects be taken which may be expected to leave the civilian population with such inadequate food or water as to cause its starvation or force its movement.[391] This language sounds very familiar to the terminology of the law of contraband which distinguishes between absolute and conditional contraband. The latter category is subject to seizure and condemnation or destruction only if found destined for the armed forces of the enemy or other hostile purposes. With respect to the law of contraband Art. 54 of Protocol I amounts to the following restrictions: Objects indispensable to the survival of the civilian population must not be declared or treated as absolute contraband. Foodstuffs and drinking water must not be treated as conditional contraband even if they are used by the enemy in direct support of military action, provided that their seizure and condemnation may leave the civilian population with such inadequate supplies as to cause its starvation or force its movement. As a matter of unavoidable consequence the arguments, put forward by *Winston Churchill* that fats are used to make explosives, potatoes make the alcohol for gasoline and plastic materials for airplane construction are made of milk — clearly a support for military operations — are no longer valid.[392]

---

[388] O. R. (note 224) vol. III, 216.

[389] *Op. cit.*, 218.

[390] *Op. cit.* vol. XV, 349.

[391] Art. 54 par. 2.

[392] See, *supra*, 89—90.

Waldemar Solf, again, seems to be the only author to have addressed this problem. He reaches the conclusion, too, that Protocol I modifies the law relevant to contraband by extending the types of supplies which cannot be considered to be contraband.[393]

[393] *Bothe* (note 358), 338, footnote 9; again, for him this is the result of the articles on relief action in Section II of Part IV, not of Art. 49 and 54 of Protocol I.

VIII. Submarine Warfare

The ramifications of Protocol I on the law of naval warfare, particularly measures against merchant ships, will not be restricted to submarine warfare. By focusing attention on this weapon in the maritime theater, however, the problems involved may become more comprehensible. It was the German unrestricted submarine warfare, waged in both World Wars that contributed to the same extent as the "adaptation" of the law of blockade and the law of contraband to the new conditions by the Entente Powers and the Allies to the withering away of the traditional distinction between civilian objects and military objectives, civilians and combatants, civilian needs and military needs.

1. Legal Regime

It may suffice for the purpose of this paper to spell out again the rules which by the majority of writers are considered as being in force, without prejudging the legal situation during World War I. When the CDDH adopted Protocol I in 1977 the rules applicable to submarine warfare were layed down in the London Naval Protocol of 6 November 1936, which provides:

1. In their action with regard to merchant ships submarines must conform to the rules of international law to which surface vessels are subject.

2. In particular, except in the case of persistent refusal to stop on being duly summoned, or of active resistance to visit and search a warship, whether surface vessel or submarine, may not sink or render incapable of navigation a merchant vessel without having first placed passengers, crew and ship's papers in a place of safety. For this purpose the ship's boats are not regarded as a place of safety, unless the safety of the passengers and crew is assured in the existing sea and weather conditions by the proximity of land, or the presence of another vessel which is in position to take them aboard.[394]

Without intention to dig deeper into the problem whether such rules can be presumed to have been legally binding already during World War I and whether they are binding at present at least for those parties

[394] See, *supra*, 13, 59.

who have ratified the London Protocol of 1936, the positions of the Manuals of Naval Warfare of the two superpowers deserve to be mentioned. The United States *Law of Naval Warfare* deals with the London Protocol of 1936 exclusively in a footnote and introduces this note with the words: "According to the customary and conventional law of naval warfare valid prior to World War II ..."[395] The *Voenno-morskoj meždunarodno-pravovoj spravočnik* of the Soviet navy strikes a similar note of caution in stressing that the London Protocol of 1936 deals with the "ideal situation of a single unarmed merchant ship on the high seas, a case where the submarine does not run the risk of being sunk by the arms of the merchant ship or by the warships or aircraft of an enemy convoy".[396]

2. State Practice

a) World War I

On 3 November 1914 Great Britain declared that the whole North Sea would be considered as a "military area" in which merchant shipping would be exposed to the gravest dangers due to the presence of mines laid by the British navy. On 4 February 1915 Germany followed suit with a Naval War Zone of her own: "Just as England declared the whole North Sea between Scotland and Norway to be comprised within the seat of war, so does Germany now declare the waters surrounding Great Britain and Ireland, including the whole English Channel, to be comprised within the seat of war, and will prevent by all the military means at its disposal all navigation by the enemy in those waters. To this end, it will endeavour to destroy, after 18 February next, any merchant vessel of the enemy which present themselves at the seat of war, above indicated, although it may not always be possible to avert the dangers which may menace persons and merchandise. Neutral powers are accordingly forewarned not to continue to entrust their crews, passengers or merchandise to such vessels. Their attention is, furthermore, called to the fact that it is of urgency to recommend to their own vessels to steer clear of these waters ..."[397]

Shortly after the start of World War I the British government had given the US government "the fullest assurances that British merchant vessels will never be used for purposes of attack, that they are merely peaceful traders armed only for defense, that they will never fire unless first fired upon and that they will never under any circumstances attack

[395] Note 21 for Chapter 5 (note 54).

[396] 455 (note 54).

[397] *Garner* (note 320) vol. I, 345, 346, 335.

any vessel".[398] In reality, the British admiralty had already issued confidential instructions which were later captured by Germany on the British steamer *Woodfield.* These instructions provided in part: "If a submarine is obviously pursuing a ship by day, and it is evident to the master that she has hostile intentions, the ship pursued should open fire in self-defense, notwithstanding the submarine may not have committed a definite hostile act, such as firing a gun or torpedo."[399] In addition, the British especially built and deployed 77 decoy ships, the so-called Q-ships, which had the appearance of an innocent merchant ship but were heavily armed and manned by Navy personnel. They were designed to lure German submarines to the surface and to destroy them. Once entrapped the U-Boats became a helpless object of attack and destruction. The Q-ships were fitted with very concealed armament which was kept hidden until the submarine was within point blank range. Then the British naval ensign was hoisted simultaneously with opening fire. This perfidy made it impossible for submarines even to try to comply with the procedures of visit and search.[400]

The attention of the world was first alarmed by the consequences of submarine warfare, when on 7 May 1915 the *Lusitania,* one of the largest British transatlantic liners was torpedoed off the English coast without warning. The *Lusitania* was armed and as all other merchant ships under the British flag had been advised by the admiralty to resist visit and search by submarines and if possible to ram them. Because the *Lusitania* carried a huge quantity of ammunition and explosives the liner sank within twenty minutes and some twelve hundred persons were drowned, 115 of them American citizens. The strongly worded US protest declared the act to be "absolutely contrary to the rules, the practices and the spirit of modern warfare" and a "violation of many sacred principles of justice and humanity".[401] Germany contended that her submarine warfare was fully authorized by the Hague Conventions and that the rules of cruiser warfare did not apply to submarine warfare, *i. e.* that submarines were not bound to give warning in order to allow the passengers time to take to the lifeboats and that the submarine was not under a legal obligation to provide for their safety.[402] In the case

[398] Papers Relating to the Foreign Relations of the United States, The World War, Washington 1929, 1916 supplement, 188.

[399] *Op. cit.,* 187, 191 *et seq.*

[400] See, the thorough analysis by *W. T. Mallison Jr.,* Submarines in General and Limited Wars, Washington 1968, in particular at 3, 4, 66, 67, 107—110.

[401] *Garner* (note 320) vol. I, 356—363.

[402] As for the German position, see in particular the collective analysis of 21 German Professors: Der Lusitania-Fall im Urteile von deutschen Gelehrten. Mit Abdruck der amtlichen Unterlagen, in: ZVR vol. IX (1916), 133—273. The authors included *Profs. Fleischmann, Binding, Hatschek, Kohler, Laband, Strupp*

of submarine warfare the Entente Powers, who themselves completely abrogated the Declaration of London and all other rules of customary international law concerning blockade and contraband insisted that the Central Powers had to abide by the traditional rules of naval warfare conceived in the time of sail and in general only with difficulties applicable to modern surface warships, not to mention submarines which could not have been dreamed of when these rules were accepted.

On 18 January 1916 the US Secretary of State *Lansing* submitted a proposal to the British government to "bring submarine warfare within the general rules of international law and the principles of humanity without destroying its efficiency in the destruction of commerce".[403] The diplomatic note observed: "I should add that my government is impressed with the reasonableness of the argument that a merchant vessel carrying an armament of any sort, in view of the character of submarine warfare and the defensive weakness of undersea craft, should be held to be an auxiliary cruiser and so treated by a neutral as well as by a belligerent government, and is seriously considering instructing its officials accordingly."[404] The US compromise proposal suggested that the Allies should disarm their merchant ships and cooperate with submarines attempting to exercise visit and search. In return, such merchant ships were not to be subjected to attack without warning and their crews and passengers should be removed to places of safety before sinking the vessels as prizes of war.[405] Because of the almost unsurmountable difficulty to bring crews and passengers to a place of safety the concessions to Germany were more specious than real. Nevertheless, Great Britain and France refused to accept this compromise proposal. Great Britain even insisted that US efforts to further advance its action would be considered as "unfriendly interference".[406]

On 10 February 1916 the US Ambassador in Berlin transmitted a German government memorandum on the treatment of armed merchant vessels to the US Secretary of State. This memorandum stated *inter alia:* "The German government has no doubt that a merchantman assumes a warlike character by armament with guns, regardless of whether the guns are intended to serve for defense or attack. It considers any warlike activity of an enemy merchantman contrary to international law, although it accords consideration to the opposite view by treating the

---

and *Triebel;* see also, *Paul Heilbron,* Der verschärfte Seekrieg, *ibid.,* 44—62, and *Franz von Liszt,* Wilson und das Völkerrecht, in: DJZ vol. 22 (1917), 256—262.

403 Foreign Relations of the United States (note 398), 1916 supplement, 146.

404 *Op. cit.,* 148.

405 *Op. cit.,* 147—148.

406 *Op. cit.,* 152—153.

crew of such a vessel not as pirates but as belligerents ... In the circumstances set forth above, enemy merchantmen armed with guns no longer have any right to be considered as peaceable vessels of commerce. Therefore, the German naval forces vill receive orders, within a short period, paying consideration to the interests of the neutrals, to treat such vessels as belligerents."[407] *Count Bernstorff*, on 8 March 1916, in another memorandum to the US government argued that the submarine is "a new weapon, the use of which had never been regulated by international law" and that its use as a matter of consequence "could not and did not violate any existing law".[408]

To be sure, the US position changed completely upon its entry into the war at the side of the Allies. The reasons were alleged German violations of the law of naval warfare. President *Wilson* in his address to the Congress on 2 April 1916 recommending a declaration of war against Germany stated *inter alia:* "The new (German) policy has swept every restriction aside. Vessels of every kind, whatever their flag, their character, their cargo, their destination, their errand, have been ruthlessly sent to the bottom without warning and without thought of help or mercy for those on board, the vessels of friendly neutrals along with those of belligerents ... I am not now thinking of the loss of property involved, immense and serious as that is, but only of the wanton and wholesale destruction of the lives of non-combatants, men, women, and children, engaged in pursuits which have always, even in the darkest periods of modern history, been deemed innocent and legitimate. Property can be paid for; the lives of peaceful and innocent people can not be. The present German submarine warfare against commerce is a warfare against mankind."[409]

On 31 January 1917 Germany proclaimed a "barred" zone extending from the Faroe Islands to the coast of Spain, westward from France and England for about 500 miles and embracing the whole of the North Sea. Within this zone, as from 1 February 1917, "all sea traffic was to be forthwith opposed by mines and submarines". All merchant vessels entering the "barred" zone without permission were subject to being torpedoed at sight by German submarines without warning and without provision being made for the safety of their passengers.[410] This act met with protests by the Entente Powers and neutral countries. It was — as all of the submarine warfare waged by Germany — characterized as

[407] *Op. cit.*, 163—165.

[408] *Garner* (note 320) vol. I, 376.

[409] Foreign Relations of the United States (note 398), 1917 supplement, No. 1, 195, 196.

[410] *Colombos*, Law of Prize (note 314), 272, 273; *Garner* (note 320) vol. I, 337, 338.

shocking inhumanity and a violation of fundamental principles of international law.[411]

In the Versailles Treaty the German government was forced to recognize the right of the Entente Powers to bring before military tribunals persons accused of having committed acts in violation of the laws and customs of war. Furthermore, the German government had to agree to hand over all persons accused of having committed such crimes.[412] *Lloyd George*, on 8 April 1919, qualified the German unrestricted submarine warfare before the Paris Peace Conference as "piracy" and the *Commission des responsabilités des auteurs de la guerre et sanctions* of the Conference put the destruction of merchant and passenger ships without warning and without provision for the safety of crew and passengers as No. 21 on the list of war crimes. After some debate the British government, however, did not put the name of *Großadmiral von Tirpitz* on the list of war criminals, despite the fact that it was feared this might be interpreted as a recognition of the lawfulness of the German submarine warfare. And when the list of war criminals was handed over to the German government, there were just four commanders of submarines named, who alledgedly attacked and destroyed hospital ships.[413]

b) World War II

In this context it is of no importance, whether the German denunciation of the London Protocol of 1936 did effectively terminate the binding force of the treaty provisions.[414] On 17 August 1940 Germany declared a counter blockade against Great Britain and announced that it considered herself entitled to destroy all merchant vessels without warning in this "zone of military operations" which was established.[415]

The Allied Powers considered these methods as ruthless submarine warfare which represented the recurrent and accumulated breach of all the established principles of international law.[416] For an evenhanded judgment one has to take into consideration what the First Lord of the British admiralty had stated in the House of Commons already three months earlier, on 8 May 1940: "Therefore, we limited our operations

---

[411] *Garner* (note 320) vol. I, 376.

[412] Art. 228 of the Treaty.

[413] *Walter Schwengler*, Völkerrecht, Versailler Vertrag und Auslieferungsfrage, Stuttgart 1982, 100, 109, 339 and 341.

[414] *Ulrich Scheuner* is of the opinion that this denunciation had no effect whatsoever, see, Entwicklungen im Seekriegsrecht seit dem zweiten Weltkrieg, in: *Hans Peter Ipsen/Karl-Hartmann Necker* (eds.), Recht über See, Festschrift zum 70. Geburtstag von *Rolf Stödter*, Hamburg/Heidelberg 1979, 287—313 (296).

[415] Urkunden zum Seekriegsrecht (note 70), No. 286.

[416] *Colombos*, Law of Prize (note 314), 278.

in the Skagerrak to the submarines. In order to make this work as effective as possible, the usual restrictions which we have imposed on the actions of our submarines were relaxed. As I told the House, all German ships by day, and all ships by night were to be sunk as opportunity served."[417]

Nonetheless, after the war again "murder of persons on the seas" figured prominently in the Nuremberg indictment.[418] The German unrestricted submarine warfare was a fact. In the actual circumstances, however, the Nuremberg tribunal was not prepared to hold *Admiral Dönitz* guilty for its conduct against British merchant ships, because shortly after the outbreak of war the British admiralty, in accordance with its Handbook of Instructions of 1938 to the merchant navy, had armed its merchant vessels, in many cases had convoyed them with armed escort, had given orders to send position reports upon sighting submarines, thus integrating merchant vessels into the warning network of naval intelligence. Furthermore on 1 October 1939 the British admiralty had announced that British merchant ships had been ordered to ram U-boats if possible.[419] In addition, the International Military Tribunal took into consideration the above mentioned order of the British admiralty of 8 May 1940, according to which all vessels should be sunk at night in the Skagerrak, and the answers to interrogatories by *Admiral Nimitz* stating that unrestricted submarine warfare was carried on in the Pacific Ocean by the United States from the first day that nation had entered the war.[420]

As to the most serious charge against *Admiral Raeder* that he carried out unrestricted submarine warfare, including sinking of unarmed merchant ships, of neutrals, nonrescue and machine-gunning of survivors contrary to the London Protocol of 1936, the Tribunal made the same findings as it did regarding *Admiral Dönitz*.[421]

3. Protocol I

The analysis of Protocol I is based upon the validity of the following assumption of the Nuremberg tribunal when it was faced with the argument of the defense that the security of the submarine is, as the first rule of the sea, paramount to rescue, and that the development of

[417] Parliamentary Debates, House of Commons, vol. 360, 1353; Urkunden zum Seekriegsrecht (note 70), No. 31.

[418] See, Judgment (note 3), 174.

[419] *Op. cit.*, 304.

[420] *Op. cit.*, 305.

[421] *Op. cit.*, 308.

aircraft made rescue impossible: "This may be so, but the Protocol (of 1936) is explicit. If the commander cannot rescue, then under its terms he cannot sink a merchant vessel and should allow it to pass harmless before his periscope."[422]

This situation does involve the life of civilians, but not the civilian population or individual civilians on land. Hence only par. 4 of Art. 49 is applicable, making the provisions of Section I of Part IV additional to the London Naval Protocol of 1936. According to the result of our interpretational efforts all other conventional or customary rules of law concerning belligerent action against military objectives at sea, which do not concern humanitarian protection, are not affected by Art. 49 and consequently this Section of Protocol I.[423] Thus Protocol I of 1977 does not contribute anything to solving the problem whether the belligerent practice in World Wars I and II of establishing "operational zones" or "war zones" is justified in the future. Such zones were barred to neutral shipping and within its boundaries belligerents claimed the right to make all ships entering the zone after notification liable to destruction at sight by submarines or aircraft.[424] This is one example of the law of naval warfare, not touched or influenced by the work of the CDDH.

Now we are clearly faced with the question, which created trouble and difficulties for some delegates at the CDDH during the second session, what the word "additional" in Art. 49 par. 4 Protocol I really means. At first glance it seems perfectly understandable that Art. 51 and 52 have to be complied with by the submarine commander. In other words, the merchant ship as a civilian object and the crew aboard as non-combatant civilians must not be made the object of an attack. Attack means an act of violence, however, "against the adversary".[425] Under the traditional law of naval warfare, including the London Protocol of 1936, a neutral merchant ship can be attacked if it persistently refuses to stop on being duly summoned or actively resists to visit and search. But is such an attack directed against the adversary within the meaning of Protocol I? Or is it directed against the neutral flag State? This has nothing to do with the "on land" problem in Art. 49 par. 3 of Protocol I, the language in par. 4 is rather clearcut. Nevertheless it seems as if the drafters had no knowledge of the law of naval warfare at all.

---

[422] *Op. cit.*, 305.

[423] See, *supra*, 60.

[424] The Nuremberg Tribunal held that this practice was a violation of the London Protocol of 1936, because this treaty had been entered into with full knowledge that such zones had been employed in the first World War without making any exceptions for operational zones; see, Judgment (note 3), 304.

[425] Art. 49 par. 1 Protocol I.

Or let us take another example. If a merchant vessel is armed and directed to ram submarines, are the precautionary measures of Protocol I, nevertheless, applicable? It would go beyond the scope of this paper to elaborate on the delicate and rather ambiguous relationship between Art. 51 and Art. 57 of Protocol I. It might suffice to say that the former is a substantive rule whilst the latter may be best described as being of a procedural nature. It comes as a surprise indeed that the procedural Article 57 on precautionary measures makes an explicit reference to naval warfare. Art. 57 par. 4 stipulates that in the conduct of military operations at sea each Party to the conflict shall, in conformity with its rights and duties under the rules of international law applicable in armed conflict, take all reasonable precautions to avoid losses of civilian lives and damage to civilian objects. Two preliminary remarks are in order. The first is called for by the language "military operations" which, obviously, has a broader connotation than "attack" in Art. 51 and 52 of Protocol I.[426] This term is not restricted to ship-to-ship combat or ship-to-air combat or attacks from the sea against objectives on land. It includes all acts committed in connection with belligerent interference with the enemy or neutral commerce, namely capture, seizure, visit and search, destruction, pursuit of blockade-runners and other measures of enforcing a naval blockade. Significantly, this broader term permits the inclusion of operations against neutral shipping, since there is no inherent limitation to acts against the adversary. The second remark pertains to the fact that this treaty article presupposes a legitimate military operation. As far as the reasonable precautions are concerned, Art. 57 par. 4 requires them "in conformity with" the existing international law. There is only one interpretation admissible, *i. e.* to read this provision as a mere repetition of an existing body of law. But if this is the case, then we have an evident contradiction at hand between this stipulation and Art. 49 par. 4 which speaks of "additional" provisions to customary and conventional rules relating to the protection of civilians and civilian objects at sea. Normally, one would not expect a codification conference to draft rules which do not have a meaning of their own. And an additional treaty rule stands on its own, even if previous conventional rights and obligations are repealed. In contrast, the mere reference in Art. 57 par. 4 makes all precautionary measures dependent upon the law as it stood before 1977. It seems ludicrous to formally declare in the basic rule that all provisions of this Section are additional and at the same time couch the least important stipulation that way.

---

[426] Par. 1 of Art. 57 also speaks of "military operations", in contrast to this par. 2, 3 and 5 refer to "attacks" as defined in Art. 49 par. 1.

In my opinion Art. 57 par. 4 is superfluous, unnecessary and confusing and has no legal effect at all. *Waldemar Solf* seems to share this point of view, but exacerbates the interpretative difficulties by adding that the inclusion of this paragraph tended to satisfy those delegations which felt uneasy about the limitations of the scope of this Section of Protocol I to the effects of attacks on objectives on land,[427] which clearly is not the case.[428] Such an evaluation can be contributed not only to a wrong conception of Art. 49 par. 3 by some CDDH delegates, but also to a complete neglect of Art. 49 par. 4. It seems to be one of the rare occasions where it is justified or even required not to further scrutinize a new provision or to attempt to reconcile it with the other content of the treaty, but to simply disregard it as an example of extremely bad draftmanship. The odd result remains, however, that a meaningless provision was inserted (Art. 57 par. 4) in order to quiet concerns about the limited scope of another provision (Art. 49 par. 3) whereas the problem was addressed in quite an unlimited fashion in a different stipulation (Art. 49 par. 4) which should have calmed down any uneasiness about the scope of application of Protocol I with respect to naval warfare.

---

427 *Bothe/Partsch/Solf* (note 241), 369.

428 See, *supra*, 57—66.

IX. Mine Warfare

The anti-ship mines presently utilized fall into four categories: physical-contact, depression, magnetic and acoustic mines. Contact mines are either moored or free-floating and explode on impact. Depression, magnetic and acoustic mines, in contrast, always rest on or are secured to the ocean floor. These mines are sensitive to fluctuations in hydrostatic pressure or changes in surrounding magnetic or acoustic energy levels. Of a different nature are more sophisticated devices which are improving rapidly in the era of emerging technologies. There are "mines" which consist of an encapsulated torpedo, which is moored to the ocean floor and can take the explosives to the enemy ship. The US Navy, *e. g.*, uses a weapon called the *Captor* mine. It does not attack surface vessels and is specifically designed for anti-submarine warfare. The *Captor* contains a *MK-46* torpedo with an active and/or passive homing device. It detects the presence of a submarine and releases the torpedo which delivers a terminally guided warhead. The sensor target acquisition radius of the *Captor* has been estimated at 1 to 3 kilometers which makes it a weapon directed in particular at deep-diving enemy submarines.[429] Other modern mines like the *Quick-strike* mines are highly sophisticated air-delivered mines with greatly improved counter-countermeasures; another marvel of modern technology is the submarine-launched mobile mile *(SLMM)*. Depending on who controls the waters being mined, one can distinguish between offensive, defensive, and protective mine warfare. The placing of mines in enemy territorial waters or waters under the control of the enemy is called offensive mining, the most effective mine warfare mission. Only the two superpowers have a full across-the-board offensive mining capability. Defensive mining is the mining of international waters and choke points not controlled by either belligerent. Protective mining is the mining of friendly territorial waters to protect ports, harbors, roadsteads, anchorages, coasts and coastal shipping routes.[430]

---

[429] Anti-Submarine Warfare, in: SIPRI Yearbook 1974, World Armaments and Disarmament, 319, 331; *C. F. Horne*, New Role for Mine Warfare, in: USNIP 1982, No. 11, 34—40; *Rex J. Zedalis*, Military Uses of Ocean Space and the Developing International Law of the Sea: An Analysis in the Context of Peacetime ASW, in: San Diego Law Review vol. 16 (1979), 576—664 (591).

[430] *Horne* (note 429).

1. Legal Regime

The only restrictions governing the belligerent employment of mines are laid down in the Hague Convention No. VIII of 18 October 1907 concerning the Laying of Automatic Submarine Contact Mines.[431] According to this Convention it is forbidden:

— to lay unanchored automatic contact mines, except when they are so constructed as to become harmless one hour at most after the person who laid them ceased to control them;[432]

— to lay anchored automatic contact mines which do not become harmless as soon as they have broken loose from their moorings;[433]

— to lay automatic contact mines off the coast and ports of the enemy, with the sole object of intercepting commercial shipping.[434]

When anchored automatic contact mines are employed every possible precaution must be taken for the security of peaceful shipping. The belligerents are obliged to do their utmost to render these mines harmless within a limited time, and, should they cease to be under surveillance, to notify the danger zones as soon as military exigencies permit, by a notice addressed to ship-owners, which must also be communicated to the governments through the diplomatic channel.[435] It may be added that Hague VIII requires that neutral powers which lay automatic contact mines off their coasts must observe the same rules and take the same precautions as are imposed on belligerents.[436] At the close of the war, the contracting Powers must do their utmost to remove the mines which they have laid, each Power removing its own mines.[437]

The apologetic preamble of Hague VIII indicates already that the Hague Peace Conference of 1907 could reach a compromise only on the smallest common denominator: "Seeing that, although the existing position of affairs makes it impossible to forbid the employment of automatic submarine contact mines, it is nevertheless desirable to restrict and regulate their employment in order to mitigate the severity of war and to ensure, as far as possible, to peaceful navigation the security to which it is entitled, despite the existence of war."[438] Indeed, given

---

431 *Hinz/Rauch* (note 1), No. 1528.
432 Art. 1 par. 1.
433 Art. 1 par. 2.
434 Art. 2.
435 Art. 3.
436 Art. 4.
437 Art. 5.
438 Par. 2 of the preamble.

the storm of hostile criticism after the first extensive use of minefields on the high seas in the Russo—Japanese War of 1904—1905, the result looks rather meager. The delegation of Colombia, *e.g.*, had proposed the following rules: "The employment of anchored contact mines is absolutely forbidden except as a means of defense.

Belligerents may not employ such mines except for the protection of their own coasts and only within a distance of the greatest range of cannon.

In the case of arms of the sea or navigable maritime channels leading exclusively to the shores of a single Power, that Power may bar the entrance for its own protection by laying anchored automatic contact mines.

Belligerents are absolutely forbidden to lay anchored automatic contact mines in the open sea or in the waters of the enemy."[439] When put to a vote 16 states voted in favor and 15 against this amendment. There were 6 abstentions and 7 absent. As the majority was not absolute the amendment failed.[440] The position of the participating states at the Hague Peace Conference were dictated by strategic advantages or disadvantages of geography. Great Britain, to be sure, was keen on achieving a complete ban of the new weapon which threatened its superiority at sea. Geographically disadvantaged states like Germany were naturally opposed to a total prohibition. Thus the Conference could agree only on some basic principles. The obligations "to take every possible precaution", "to do their utmost to render these mines harmless within a limited time" or to notify the danger zones "as soon as military exigencies permit" are not much more than guidelines which leave broad room for discretion. The same holds true with respect to the prohibition to lay automatic contact mines off the coast and ports of the enemy with the "sole object" of intercepting commercial shipping. This stipulation has to be read in the context of the requirement of effectiveness for a lawful naval blockade, which cannot be simply met by deploying mines in order to render passage of merchant vessels dangerous. It has even been doubtful whether a belligerent is permitted to use mines as a supplementary means for enforcing an otherwise lawful blockade.[441] But a belligerent has only to proclaim that it is not his "sole" intention to intercept merchant shipping and his actions do not run afoul of Hague VIII. Strangely enough, the most important result of this Convention seems to have been the removal of any doubts about the legality of the laying of mines upon the high seas. Together

---

[439] *Scott* (note 83) vol. I, 285; vol. III, annex 36.

[440] *Op. cit.* vol. I, 286.

[441] *Tucker* (note 314), 298.

with the discretionary measures indicated above Hague VIII has to be construed as prohibiting only mine-laying of an openly indiscriminate character, *e. g.* without any regard to definite military operations and without any reasonable control or surveillance.[442]

For a final assessment of the Convention, I may be permitted to quote the statements made by the representatives of Great Britain and Germany on 9 October 1907. After the horrors of two World Wars they sound almost like coming from another planet. *Sir Ernest Satow* stated: "(The British delegation) does not consider that adequate account has been taken in the Convention of the right of neutrals to protection, or of humanitarian sentiments which cannot be neglected ... We declare without hesitation that the right of the neutral to security of navigation on the high seas ought to come before the transitory right of the belligerent to employ these seas as the scene of operations of war. Nevertheless, the Convention as adopted imposes upon the belligerent no restriction as to the placing of anchored mines, which consequently may be laid wherever the belligerent chooses, in his own waters for self-defense, in the waters of the enemy as a means of attack, or finally on the high seas, so that neutral navigation will inevitably run great risks in time of naval war, and may be exposed to many a disaster ... We did not fail to bring forward every argument in favor of limiting the field of action for these mines, while we called very special attention to the advantages which the civilized world would gain from this restriction ... But, since the Conference has not shared our views, it remains for us to declare in the most formal manner that these dangers exist, and that the certainty that they will make themselves felt in the future is due to the incomplete character of the present Convention. As this Convention, in our opinion, constitutes only a partial and inadequate solution of the problem, it cannot, as has already been pointed out, be regarded as a complete exposition of the international law on this subject. Accordingly, it will not be permissible to presume the legitimacy of an action for the mere reason that this Convention has not prohibited it. This is a principle which we desired to affirm and which it will be impossible for any State to ignore, whatever its power."[443] *Baron Marschall von Bieberstein* repeated what he had already said in the Commission: "That a belligerent who lays mines assumes a very heavy responsibility towards neutrals and towards peaceful shipping is a point on which we all agreed. No one will resort to this instrument of warfare unless for military reasons of an absolutely urgent character. But military acts are not solely governed by

---

[442] *Op. cit.*, 303.

[443] *Scott* (note 83) vol. I, 274, 275.

stipulations of international law. There are other factors: Conscience, good sense, and the sentiment of duty imposed by principles of humanity will be the surest guides for the conduct of sailors and will constitute the most effective guaranty against abuses. The officers of the German navy, I loudly proclaim it, will always fulfill in the strictest fashion the duties which emanate from the unwritten law of humanity and civilization. I have no need to tell you that I entirely recognize the importance of the codification of rules to be followed in war. But it would be a great mistake to issue rules the strict observance of which might be rendered impossible by the law of facts. It is of the first importance that the international maritime law which we desire to create should only contain clauses the execution of which is possible from a military point of view — is possible even in exceptional circumstances. Otherwise the respect for law would be lessened and its authority undermined."[444]

Anchored and unanchored automatic contact mines are not exactly the most modern and sophisticated mines. Thus the first question to be answered is whether Hague VIII can be applied by way of analogy to other mines as well. And in this context what was considered a shortcoming in 1907 might prove to be an advantage. Since the Convention restricts itself to some basic principles they lend themselves to application *mutatis mutandis* to similar weapon systems created by new technological developments despite the fact that they were not contemplated by the drafters of these rules. The Soviet Manual of Naval Warfare contents itself with repeating the language of Hague VIII.[445] The Manual of the United States Navy, however, in a footnote emphasizes that the "general purpose" of the Convention provisions must be considered in arriving at any extrapolation of the Hague Rules to serve as a guide to lawful conduct with respect to weapons, not specifically covered by these provisions, such as magnetic and acoustic mines.[446] It is my considered opinion that the use of any depression, magnetic and acoustic mines has to be compatible with the rules established in Hague VIII for automatic contact mines — *mutatis mutandis.*[447] More important, however, are new devices that remain innocuous until automatically or remotely activated. I do not see how they can be brought under the purview of Hague VIII. If this activation is achieved automatically there may be a possibility for an analogous application of the provisions for the time after actual activation. Care should be taken in this respect, however, not to generalize. The problem

[444] *Op. cit.*, 275, 276.

[445] USSR NILM (note 54), 450—454.

[446] US LNW (note 54), 6—8, note 3 for chapter 6.

[447] See also, *Tucker* (note 314), 304, footnote 49.

is very sensitive and much depends upon how modern technology works. In the final analysis responsible decisions can be rendered only on a case by case basis. Even more difficult problems arise with respect to weapon systems like the *Captor* mine mentioned above. Despite its denomination this device is not a mine within the meaning of the legal term of art. Legally it is a torpedo with a terminally guided warhead. Its use has to be in accordance with the special provision of Hague VIII forbidding the employment of torpedoes which do not become harmless when they have missed their mark.[448] An analogy to the rules for mines seems too far-fetched because of the operative characteristics and functional attributes of such devices.

2. State Practice

A brief survey of the actual mine warfare by the belligerents in both World Wars seems in order to prepare a correct evaluation of the repercussions of the LOS Convention and of Protocol I.

a) World War I

On the very first day of World War I the German cruiser *Königin Luise* was sunk by British forces while engaged in laying mines in the open waters of the North Sea. In the following weeks several British warships as well as merchant vessels and merchantmen of neutral nations were sunk at sea by German mines. On 23 August 1914 the British admiralty issued the following warning: "The Germans are continuing their practice of scattering mines indiscriminately upon the ordinary trade routes. These mines do not become harmless after a certain number of hours; they are not laid in connection with any definite military scheme, such as the closing of a military port, or as a distinct operation against an invading fleet, but appear to be scattered on the chance of touching individual British war or merchant vessels." The London Times protested against this "callous and inhumane mode of warfare" and in the House of Lords the British admiralty was asked "to counteract the inhuman and diabolical German practice of sowing mines broadcast on the commercial routes at sea". One member of the House of Lords stated that "such mine-laying is not war, but a barbarous attempt at indiscriminate murder".[449]

On 2 October 1914 the British government announced that it deemed it necessary to adopt counter-measures and gave notice that it would be dangerous for ships to pass through the area between 51°15′ and

[448] Art. 1 par. 3.

[449] *Garner* (note 320) vol. I, 329, 330.

51°40′ north latitude and 1°35′ and 3°00′ east longitude.[450] The Dutch coast-guard picked up more than a dozen mines per day that had broken from their moorings and drifted upon the Netherlands' coast. Charges and counter-charges that they were German or British mines freely floating in the North Sea escalated. The German ambassador to Washington presented a memorandum to the State Department in which he affirmed that the German mines were of a type which became harmless when they broke loose. Accusations and counter-accusations also concerned the use of fishing vessels and merchant vessels flying a neutral flag for mine laying.[451]

On 3 November 1914 Great Britain established the first War Zone, which has been already mentioned above.[452] The order read in part: "Owing to the discovery of mines in the North Sea, the whole of that sea must be considered a military area. Within this area merchant shipping of all kinds, traders of all countries, fishing craft, and all other vessels will be exposed to the gravest dangers from mines which it has been necessary to lay and from warships searching vigilantly by night and day for suspicious craft. All merchant and fishing vessels of every description are hereby warned of the dangers they encounter by entering this area except in strict accordance with admiralty directions."[453] The War Zone was justified as an "exceptional measure, appropriate to the novel conditions under which this war is being carried on".[454]

By way of retaliation Germany issued the War Zone Decree of 4 February 1915, which has been already mentioned and quoted in the context of blockade and contraband.[455] In May 1916, Great Britain extended the British minefields in the straits of Dover so as to include the waters south of latitude 51°40′ and north as far as the meridian of 3°20′ east. In January 1917, the British War Zone in the North Sea was greatly extended; it virtually enclosed the whole area between Germany and England except for the marginal territorial seas of Denmark and the Netherlands. It was not expressly admitted, but inferred that mines would be used indiscriminately in that "danger zone".[456] During the same month Germany promulgated the "Barred" Zone Decree, according to which in the whole of the North Sea and parts of the Atlantic "all sea traffic was to be forthwith opposed by mines and submarines".[457]

[450] *Op. cit.*, 332.

[451] *Op. cit.*, 331, 332.

[452] See, *supra*, 83—84, 103.

[453] *Garner* (note 320) vol. I, 333.

[454] *Ibid.*

[455] Quoted *supra*, 103.

[456] *Garner* (note 320) vol. I, 334.

In the last three months of 1917 alone Great Britain laid over 10,000 mines in the German Bight and the Strait of Dover solely for the purpose of destroying some of the German submarines. In 1918, in addition to further very extensive mining in these two areas, some 100,000 mines were laid in the North Sea Barrage by the British navy against German submarines.[458]

Neutral powers protested vigorously against this practice of mine laying by the two belligerents.[459]

On 20 February 1915 the United States government had addressed an identical communication to Great Britain and Germany as a "sincere friend desirous of embarrassing neither nation involved and of serving, if it may, the common interests of humanity". The US suggested that Germany and Great Britain agree to abstain from sowing floating mines on the high seas, except within cannon range of harbors for defensive purposes only; and that all mines should bear the stamp of the government planting them and should be so constructed as to become harmless if separated from their moorings. The German government replied in a note dated 1 March 1915 and agreed to abandon the use of floating mines and to use only anchored mines constructed as suggested by the United States. However, it insisted that it did not appear feasible for belligerents to forego completely the deployment of anchored mines for offensive purposes. Great Britain answered that it did not understand from the reply of the German government that Germany was prepared to abandon the use of mines for offensive purposes on the high seas. This being so, it was not necessary to make any further reply.[460]

b) World War II

Germany and Great Britain used mines extensively throughout the war. Both sides declared their first minefields immediately upon the outbreak of hostilities and continued this practice until the cessation of the fighting.[461] In the initial stages of the war Great Britain charged

[457] See, *supra*, 106.

[458] *Mallison* (note 400), 5.

[459] *Garner* (note 320) vol. I, 339—341.

[460] *Op. cit.*, 347—349.

[461] Germany declared minefields on 1 September 1939, 3 and 5 September 1939, 9 April 1940, 10 May 1940 and 18 May 1940 *e. g.* in the Baltic, North Sea, North Atlantic and off the South-African ports, see, Urkunden zum Seekriegsrecht (note 70), Nos. 339—357; Great Britain *e. g.* declared minefields on 3 September 1939, 12, 17 and 22 September 1939, 18 October 1939, 1 and 24 December 1940, 8 April 1940, 14 and 28 April 1940, July 1940 in the Strait of Dover, Firth of Forth, German Bight, North Sea, Skagerrak and Kattegat, Baltic and North Atlantic (Orkney-Islands, Iceland, Greenland), see, Urkunden zum Seekriegsrecht (note 70), Nos. 361—379.

that Germany had violated the provisions of Hague VIII by the indiscriminate laying of mines along the paths of the principal trade routes, by failure to notify peaceful shipping of the precise extent of the minefields, and by laying mines off the English coast for the sole purpose of interrupting neutral shipping. Germany denied these charges and maintained that the notification of minefields according to the Hague Convention depended upon military considerations which Germany alone could judge and that the purpose of laying minefields off the English coast was not for the "sole purpose" of intercepting commercial shipping.[462]

On 17 August 1940 Germany announced the "total blockade" of Great Britain. The announcement concluded: "The government of the *Reich* wishes to emphasize the following fact: The naval war in the waters around the British Isles is in full progress. The whole area has been mined."[463]

There were a lot of diplomatic exchanges with neutral countries whose merchant vessels were sunk by mines.[464] And many of the measures taken by the belligerents were protested against.[465] According to the Soviet Manual of Naval Warfare at least 1 million sea mines were used during World War II. The Manual neither states nor implies that this practice was a violation of international law.[466]

3. Law of the Sea Convention

As far as the new LOS Convention is concerned, the regime for military installations and structures on the continental shelf and in the EEZ of other states has to be scrutinized as to whether it has an impact on the law of mine warfare on the continental shelf or in the EEZ of neutral states.[467]

The EEZ includes the sea-bed and subsoil of the 200 nm belt, which is dealt with in the Convention by a cross-reference to the legal regime

[462] See, Urkunden zum Seekriegsrecht (note 70), Nos. 323, 324 and 325.

[463] US Naval War College, International Law Documents, Newport R. I. 1940, 46—50.

[464] See, the diplomatic exchanges with neutral countries concerning the sinking of vessels, Urkunden zum Seekriegsrecht (note 70), Nos. 326, 327, 328, 418 (Argentina), Nos. 329 and 330 (Norway), Nos. 331, 332 (Japan) and Nos. 333, 334, 335, 336, 337, 338 (Netherlands).

[465] See, the diplomatic protests by Sweden and Norway, Urkunden zum Seekriegsrecht (note 70), Nos. 352 and 373.

[466] USSR NILM (note 54), 452—454.

[467] As to the EEZ in general, see, supra, 33—38, since the LOS Convention contains a special regime for artificial islands, installations and structures in the EEZ we have to analyze this problem separately from the general situation regarding military uses in this zone of national jurisdiction.

of the continental shelf.[468] The continental shelf of a coastal state, in turn, extends to the outer limit of the EEZ even in those cases where the outer edge of the continental margin does not extend up to that distance.[469] If the natural prolongation of the coastal state's land territory reaches beyond the 200 mile line, we have a continental shelf within the meaning of the 1958 Convention on the Continental Shelf,[470] *i. e.* a submarine area the superjacent waters of which form part of the high seas.[471] The legal regime of military installations on the outer continental shelf and on the sea-bed, subsoil, water column and surface of the EEZ is identical. Thus the Convention avails itself of the technique to spell out this regime in Part V on the EEZ[472] and to make another cross-reference in Part VI on the continental shelf.[473]

The 1958 Convention on the Continental Shelf did not address the problem of military uses at all. The coastal state was given exclusive jurisdiction for the purpose of exploring it and exploiting its natural resources.[474] As a matter of consequence all military uses remained subject to the high seas regime which used to be applicable to the shelf areas beyond the territorial sea before the 1958 Convention entered into force.[475] There was, however, one exception, concerning marine scientific research undertaken on the shelf and concerning the shelf. This research, whether for civilian or military purposes was subject to the coastal state's consent.[476] For instance, drilling on the continental shelf in order to conduct feasibility studies for the emplacement of mines was lawful only upon the express consent of the coastal state. At UNCLOS I in 1958 India had presented a proposal stipulating that "the continental shelf adjacent to any coastal state shall not be used by the coastal state or any other state for the purpose of building military bases or installations".[477] This proposal was defeated by 31 votes to 18 with 6 abstentions.[478] This proves that before UNCLOS III the coastal state as well as all other states enjoyed the freedom to emplace military installations on the continental shelf.

---

468 Art. 56 par. 3.

469 Art. 76 par. 1.

470 UNTS vol. 499 (1964), 311.

471 Art. 3 of the 1958 Convention.

472 Art. 60.

473 Art. 80; there is one exception, however, since Art. 59 applies only to the continental shelf within the 200 nm EEZ and not to the outer continental shelf.

474 Art. 2; see, Art. 77 par. 1 of the LOS Convention.

475 UNTS (note 470).

476 Art. 5 par. 8.

477 O. R. (note 224) vol. V, 141.

478 *Op. cit.* vol. VI, 91.

This position was forcefully corroborated by the 1971 Sea-Bed Treaty[479] which presupposes the lawful use of the continental shelf of all states for the emplacement of military equipment for surveillance and verification equipment.[480] This issue gave rise to many conflicting statements of understanding during the negotiations and even on the occasion of signing or ratifying the treaty. During the debate preceding the adoption of the Sea-Bed Treaty several countries expressed the opinion that no state may construct, operate, or maintain any installations — whether civilian or military — on the continental shelf of another state without the latter's consent.[481] The co-sponsors of the draft treaty were forced to make a number of changes in the text and even to include a special disclaimer clause in order to smooth the way for a consensus.[482] The two superpowers repeatedly had to declare that the Sea-Bed Treaty was designed solely to accomplish the purpose that it was designed to serve — namely, to prevent the extension of the race in nuclear and other weapons of mass destruction to the sea-bed and that the treaty was not intended to solve numerous questions of the law of the sea.[483] But there were, nevertheless, quite a number of statements which were tantamount to a reservation. Canada accompanied its deposit of the instrument of ratification with the declaration that the treaty cannot be interpreted as indicating that any state has a right to implant or emplace any weapons not prohibited by the treaty on the continental shelf, or on the sea-bed and ocean floor or in the subsoil thereof. Furthermore nothing in the treaty can be interpreted as indicating any restrictions or limitations upon the rights of the coastal state to verify, inspect or effect the removal of any weapon, structure, installation, facility or device implanted or emplaced on the continental shelf, or the subsoil thereof, appertaining to that coastal state.[484] India made a declaration accompanying accession to the effect

[479] See, *supra*, 11.

[480] See, Art. III par. 6.

[481] UN Doc. A/C. 1/PV 1763 of 17 November 1970.

[482] Art. IV: "Nothing in this Treaty shall be interpreted as supporting or prejudicing the position of any State Party with respect to existing international conventions, including the 1958 Convention on the Territorial Sea and the Contiguous Zone, or with respect to rights or claims which such State Party may assert, or with respect to recognition or nonrecognition of rights or claims asserted by any other state, related to waters of its coasts including, *inter alia*, territorial seas and contiguous zones, or to the seabed and the ocean floor, including continental shelves."

[483] These statements of the two superpowers were quoted by Argentina in a declaration on signature, that they constitute the true interpretation of the treaty and that it is with that understanding that the government of Argentina signs the instrument, see, Status of Multilateral Arms Regulation and Disarmament Agreements, Special Supplement to the UN Disarmament Yearbook vol. II (1977), New York 1978, 107.

[484] *Op cit.*, 108—109.

that other countries cannot use its continental shelf for military purposes and continued: "There cannot, therefore, be any restriction on, or limitation of, the sovereign right of India as a coastal state to verify, inspect, remove or destroy any weapon, device, structure, installation or facility, which might be emplanted or emplaced on or beneath its continental shelf by any other country, or to take such other steps as may be considered necessary to safeguard its security."[485] The United States, in *notes verbales* dated 4 and 31 October 1972 rejected in carefully couched terms these statements.[486] India reiterated its position in a reply to the US *note verbale* dated 30 January 1974.[487] In an intervention at the 1977 Review Conference of the Sea-Bed Treaty India stated again that "other countries could not use its continental shelf for military purposes" and that India has "the sovereign right to ... verify, inspect, remove or destroy any weapon, device, structure, installation or facility which might be emplanted or emplaced on or beneath its continental shelf by any other country".[488]

At the first substantive negotiating sessions of UNCLOS III, 1974 at Caracas, Mexico and Kenya tabled a proposal which was later co-sponsored by 35 other states and stipulated that "no state shall be entitled to construct, maintain, deploy or operate on or over the continental shelf of another state any military installations or devices or any other installations for whatever purposes without the consent of the coastal state".[489] This proposal was never incorporated into any of the various negotiating texts. As a Canadian observer puts it, "the United States apparently made it clear that it would be willing to see the entire Conference collapse rather than compromise on this kind of issue".[490] Another speaks of "heavy American pressure".[491]

According to the LOS Convention the coastal state has the exclusive right to construct and to authorize and regulate the construction, operation and use of artificial islands for whatever purposes in its exclusive economic zone and on its continental shelf.[492] From these artificial

---

485 *Op. cit.*, 111.

486 *Op. cit.*, 109, 111, 113.

487 *Op. cit.*, 112; see also, *Gundolf Fahl*, Internationales Recht der Rüstungsbeschränkungen, vol. 2, Berlin 1982, No. 6.3.1.1., 11; the United States countered with a note dated 7 June 1974 in which it made reference to the note of 4 October 1973.

488 UN Doc. SBT/CONF./SR. 5 of 24 June 1977 par. 11 *et seq.*

489 UN Doc. A/CONF. 62/C. 2/L. 42/Rev. 1 of 13 August 1974.

490 *Ronald G. Purver*, Canadian Foreign Policy and the Military Use of the Seabed, in: *Barbara Johnson/Mark W. Zacher* (ed.), Canadian Foreign Policy and the Law of the Sea, Vancouver 1977, 202—254 (212).

491 *Barry Buzan*, A Sea of Troubles? Source of Dispute in the New Ocean Regime, Adelphi Papers No. 143, London 1978, 12.

492 Arts. 60 par. 1 (a), 80.

islands the Convention distinguishes "installations and structures". Here the coastal state's jurisdiction is restricted to installations and structures for the purposes provided for in Articles 56 and 77 of the Convention and other economic purposes.[493] Art. 56 for the EEZ and Art. 77 for the continental shelf attribute sovereign rights for the purposes of exploring and exploiting, conserving and managing the natural resources. Military purposes are clearly distinct from resource-related and other economic purposes. In addition to these installations and structures the coastal state has also exclusive jurisdiction regarding all installations and structures which "may interfere" with the exercise of its rights in the EEZ or on the continental shelf.[494] As in the case of artificial islands this treaty provision includes all purposes, civilian or military ones. If and when such installations and structures "may" interfere with the exercise of the coastal state's resource-oriented jurisdiction, they must not be constructed or used or operated without the consent of the coastal state. In this conflict situation the interests of the coastal state clearly prevail over *e. g.* military interests of other states.[495]

If this conflict situation does not or not yet exist the question arises what the legal situation is. The Convention is silent on this issue, consequently the law remains unchanged and all states enjoy the high seas freedom of constructing, using and operating military installations and structures on the continental shelf and in the EEZ. There are no residual rights and jurisdictions for the coastal state.[496] As an unavoidable consequence the law of the sea applies as it has been developed before the adoption of the LOS Convention, since its preamble expressly states that matters not regulated by it continue to be governed by the rules and principles of general international law. This is a reference also to the traditional high seas freedom to emplace and emplant installations and structures for military purposes which had been preserved by the 1958 Continental Shelf Convention.

In the event that after the deployment of military installations the coastal state wants to explore and exploit the natural resources in its zones of national jurisdiction it becomes important that the new LOS Convention does not expressly attribute jurisdiction over installations and structures for military purposes on the continental shelf and in the EEZ. With respect to the EEZ including the shelf up to 200 miles Art. 59

---

[493] Arts. 60 par. 1 (b), 80.

[494] Arts. 60 par. 1 (c), 80.

[495] See, *John R. Stevenson/Bernard H. Oxman,* The Third United Nations Conference on the Law of the Sea: The 1975 Geneva Session, in: AJIL vol. 69 (1975), 763—797 (777).

[496] See, *Willem Riphagen,* La navigation dans le nouveau droit de la mer, in: RGDIP vol. 84 (1980), 144—177.

of the Convention provides that in such cases, where a conflict arises between the interests of the coastal state and any other state or states, the conflict should be resolved on the basis of equity and in the light of all the relevant circumstances taking into account the respective importance of the interests involved to the parties as well as to the international community as a whole. It has to be stressed that this provision is not applicable as regards the outer continental shelf beyond 200 nautical miles. The first conclusion to be drawn from this stipulation is that the above interpretation is correct. This provision under the heading "Basis for the resolution of conflicts regarding the attribution of rights and jurisdiction in the exclusive economic zone" presupposes the freedom to construct, use and operate installations and structures for military purposes. Otherwise the conflict to be resolved would not exist. And a second observation is in order. This treaty provision is a procedural dispute settlement device and has no substantive meaning except for the implication that the rule *in dubio pro libertate* can be used as a starting point.[497] In view of the fact that the LOS Convention attributes exclusive jurisdiction with regard to all installations and structures which may interfere with the exercise of its rights to the coastal state the conflict resolution provision can be applied only in those cases where the use of a certain area of the EEZ changes in the course of time. For instance, when a state has emplanted military installations on the continental shelf of another state 180 nautical miles off the coast without any possible interference with the exercise of coastal state jurisdiction and the latter now decides to drill for gas or oil in that area. This conflict has to be resolved under Art. 59 of the Convention. The coastal state does not have a right to unilaterally remove or destroy the military installations on its shelf. The conflict of interest has to be resolved by negotiations on the basis of equity and in the light of all the relevant circumstances including the military interests of the other state.

The principal question, of course, is whether mines are installations at all within the meaning of the law of the sea. For the purpose of this paper it might suffice to say that a single mine of one type may not be an installation, but that antisubmarine mine barriers using a different type of mines might well be. The decision has to be made on a case by case basis dependent upon size, operative characteristics and functional attributes of the different types of mines, which are classified.

In summary, under the peacetime law of the sea — applicable in times of tension and crisis — the freedom to deploy mines in the EEZ and on the continental shelf of other states is restricted if they may

---

[497] *Tullio Treves,* Military Installations, Structures, and Devices on the Seabed, in: AJIL vol. 74 (1980), 808—857 (821, 822).

interfere with the exercise of the rights of the coastal state which are resource-oriented. In such a situation it is decisive when such a conflict arises. If the conflict would be created by the emplacement of mines this act would be unlawful without express consent of the coastal state.[498] If it arises after emplacement of the mines, the conflict has to be resolved according to Art. 59 of the Convention. Finally it should be emphasized that in all cases the exercise of the freedom to deploy military installations is conditional upon the state's having due regard to the rights and duties of the coastal state.[499]

In order to solve the problem whether this legal regime has any ramifications on the law of mine warfare in armed conflict at sea we have in the first place to refer to the results of our analysis concerning the EEZ in general.[500] That means we are again faced with the interdependence of sovereignty and neutrality. And neither the continental shelf nor the EEZ are under the sovereignty of the coastal state. The latter exercises only jurisdiction aimed at the exploration and exploitation of natural resources. To subject the continental shelf or the EEZ to principles of neutrality in times of war would be tantamount to an appropriation of the area concerned and an extension of coastal state sovereignty. In addition, the applicable law of war contains a safeguard for the resource-oriented interests of the coastal state in its zones of national jurisdiction which can be compared to the "due regard" and "relevant circumstance" provisions of the peacetime law of the sea.[501] The law of war version of this concept is called the principle of proportionality. Mine warfare on the continental shelf and in the EEZ of another state must not cause disproportionate collateral damage to the resource-related activities of the coastal state or to the resources itself. To phrase it in terms of Protocol I, mine warfare in the zones of national jurisdiction of other states which are not belligerent must not cause incidental loss of natural resources, whether living or non-living, oil-rigs, platforms for gas or oil storage, pipelines for the transportation of offshore oil and gas etc, which would be excessive in relation to the concrete and direct military advantage anticipated. The use of mines which may be expected to cause such collateral damage is prohibited as an act of indiscriminate warfare.[502]

Due to the special characteristics of naval warfare until now the rule of proportionality did not play an important role, except for naval

---

[498] Art. 60 par. 1 (c). It is assumed that we are dealing with mines which meet the requirements of an "installation".

[499] Art. 58 par. 3.

[500] See, *supra*, 33—38.

[501] See, Arts. 56 par. 2, 58 par. 3, 59, 87 par. 1 LOS Convention.

[502] Arts. 51 par. 5 (b), 57 par. 2 (a) (iii) and (b).

bombardments of military objectives on land. The United States Manual of Naval Warfare of 1955 did not even list this rule amongst the basic principles of the laws of war, but mentions only military necessity, humanity, chivalry and distinction between combatants and non-combatants.[503] The Draft United States Law of Naval Operations of 1982, however, deals with the principle of proportionality in the context of "proportionality and humanity" and "collateral damage".[504]

In summary, the LOS Convention of 1982 does not create any new legal restraints for mine-warfare which did not exist previously. This new treaty is important, however, because it accentuates the importance of the principle of proportionality by focusing on and extending coastal state jurisdiction over natural resources in areas adjacent to the territorial sea and under its jurisdiction ,which are not under coastal state sovereignty and therefore remain part of the maritime theater. Consequently, the impact of the new Convention on mine warfare consists in the sharpening and elaboration of the requirement that the naval commander must give more consideration to resource-oriented interests and activities on the continental shelf and in the EEZ than on the high seas and that a carefully weighed decision has to be made in each case of mine laying about the proportionality of the expected and unavoidable collateral damage.

4. Protocol I

a) Applicability

The problem concerning the applicability of the Protocol I combat provisions is twofold. First, we have again to face the implications of the "eye of the needle" in Art. 49. Second, we must answer the question whether the use of mines constitutes an attack within the meaning of Protocol I. Art. 49 (4) makes all provisions of Part IV Section I additional to the rules concerning humanitarian protection contained in international agreements binding upon the parties as well as to customary rules of international law relating to the protection of civilians and civilian objects at sea against the effects of hostilities. The Hague Convention No. VIII concerning the Laying of Automatic Submarine Contact Mines of 18 October 1907 is a treaty which meets these requirements. This is evidenced by its preamble and corroborated by the statements of the rapporteur of the first subcommission of the Third Commission which had been charged by the Second Hague Peace Conference to draft

503 US LNW (note 54), No. 220, 2—4; No. 221, 2—5.

504 Law of Naval Operations, Part I: Naval Commander's Handbook on the Law of Armed Conflict, NWP 10-1, Draft 6 July 1982, Washington D.C., at 1.2.2.1 and 3.1.3.

the mine convention. *Mr. Georgius Streit* expressly declared that "the Commission ... guided by humanitarian considerations and respect for the principle of the liberty of maritime highways, has prepared a collection of rules that are yet destined to check the horrors of war and to restrain in so far as possible the useless hardships of armed conflicts between nations".[505] The group of experts of the German Red Cross was therefore correct in mentioning Hague VIII as one of the international agreements to which the combat rules of Protocol I are additional.[506] The situation is the same as with the London Protocol of 1936 concerning submarine warfare.[507] As far as the Protocol I provisions refer to "military operations" there are no further difficulties since the laying of sea mines is such an operation.[508]

The answer is by far more difficult with respect to those stipulations which deal with "attacks". "Attacks" mean acts of violence against the adversary, whether in offense or in defense.[509] At the outset, it has to be underscored that this legal term is quite different from the notion used by the military profession. The military "attack" means fire and movement.[510] As a matter of course, sea mines as well as land mines normally cannot be a means of attack within this sense because the element of movement is lacking. Mines simply sit and wait. For the legal ramifications of Protocol I on mine warfare at sea it is interesting to note that obvious attempts have been made to get rid of this problem for the employment of land mines. On 10 October 1980 the UN Weapons Conference in Geneva adopted a Convention on Prohibitions or Restrictions on the Use of Certain Conventional Weapons which may be deemed to be Excessively Injurious or to have Indiscriminate Effects (Weapons Convention), which consists of an umbrella treaty and three annexed Protocols on Non-Detectable Fragments, on the Use of Mines, Booby-Traps and Other Devices (Mines Protocol) and on Prohibitions or

---

505 *Scott* (note 83) vol. I, 273.

506 Handbuch des Deutschen Roten Kreuzes (note 218), 156 footnote 1, 158 footnote 2.

507 See, *supra*, 108—111.

508 The term "military operations" is used, *e.g.*, in Arts. 48, 51 paras. 1, 7; 57 paras. 1, 4; 58 (c). The interpretative problems created by Art. 57 par. 4 for mine warfare are identical with those for submarine warfare, see, *supra*, 109—111.

509 Art. 49 par. 1.

510 For the armed forces of the Federal Republic of Germany the term "attack" as a military term is defined in: Heeresdienstvorschrift (HDv) 100/900, Führungsbegriffe (TF/B), Bonn 1977: "Angriff ist eine Gefechtsart, in der eine Truppe unter Raumgewinn Feindkräfte zerschlägt oder zurückwirft. Der Angriff wirkt durch Bewegung, Feuer und in die Richtung, in der er geführt wird. Er soll meist die Entscheidung des Gefechts herbeiführen. In manchen Lagen dient er nur dazu, ein bestimmtes Gelände in Besitz zu nehmen, aufzuklären, den Feind zu täuschen oder im Kampf stehende eigene Truppen zu entlasten."

Restrictions on the Use of Incendiary Weapons which form an integral part of the Convention.[511] The Mines Protocol does not use the term "attack" any more but speaks of the "use" of mines.[512]

It has been said that the emplacement or delivery of a mine is not an act of violence, because it does not harm anybody or anything at all; the act of violence is not committed by the user of the mine, but by those who cause it to detonate or explode through presence, proximity or contact. Such reasoning cannot be accepted, however. From a legal point of view it makes no difference that the emplacement or delivery of the mine alone does not trigger the violent explosion. A mine is an explosive device. And a delayed act of violence is still an act of violence.[513] Another argument has as its starting point the prerequisite that the act of violence has to be committed "against the adversary". Landmines, so the argument goes, do not meet this requirement because they are only directed against the piece of land on or in which they have been deployed in order to neutralize it.[514] If this suggestion were not perfectly specious, it would exclude all uses of sea mines from the new law of weapon restraint embodied in Protocol I. The sea mine would be directed against an area of water only which was to be denied to enemy or neutral use. Barrier, denial or protective minefields at sea in particular would never run afoul of the "attack" provisions in Protocol I. To be sure, such an "interpretation" based upon the fact that a sea mine is a delayed-action weapon and a time-fused or target-activated explosive device is not tenable and a change in the denomination of anti-ship mines to "anti-area-of-water" mines would not be helpful either. The explosive power of a sea mine is always directed against the adversary. Object and purpose of mine warfare at sea is not only the deterrence of the enemy or of neutral merchant vessels to use a certain area of the oceans, to harrass, hamper, disturb and interfere with the adversary's naval operations, but also to destroy its surface ships and submarines and to destroy merchant vessels which have become a legitimate military objective through certain activities such as blockade running, unneutral service, resistance to visit and search *etc.* Because of the technical features of a sea mine, notably the fact that the act of violence is conditioned and delayed, it is necessary to consider the laying of the mine, the activating (automatically or remotely controlled) and the explosion as one act under the law of naval warfare. To advocate a two-track approach by distinguishing between the laying (and activating) of a sea

[511] See, *Rauch* (note 274).

[512] See, Arts. 3, 4, 5 of the Mines Protocol.

[513] See, *Rauch* (note 274), 271.

[514] *Op. cit.*, 271, 272.

mine on the one hand, and the violent explosion on the other, would be tantamount to negating the responsibility for mine warfare under the law of naval warfare.[515]

b) Prohibitions and Restrictions

In accordance with Art. 49 (4) all provisions of Part IV Section I of Protocol I are applicable to mine warfare at sea as we have seen, including those dealing with "attacks". Due to the nature of such warfare the rules protecting the civilian population as such are not relevant. With this exception all prohibitions and restrictions, which have been spelled out in detail in the context of naval bombardments of military objectives on land, have to be complied with.[516] The most important of them for naval mine warfare is the prohibition of indiscriminate attacks, which for all objects and purposes marks the end of traditional mine warfare as waged in both World Wars by all belligerents. The extensive use of freely floating or moored mines without constant surveillance and control by the belligerent engaged in such warfare constitutes a forbidden indiscriminate attack. Such scattered mines and minefields are directed against military objectives, but not against a "specific" military objective as required by Art. 51 (4) (a). Furthermore, traditional sea mines are weapons and the mine warfare waged in World War I and II is a method of combat which cannot be directed at a "specific" military objective within the meaning of Art. 51 (4) (b). Consequently, in both cases, the use of mines is of a nature to strike military objectives and civilians or civilian objects without distinction. With all probability traditional mine warfare at sea also fulfills the requirements of the third category of indiscriminate attacks as defined in Art. 51 (4) (c). Sea mines are a means of combat and the laying of unobserved and uncontrolled minefields is a method of combat the effects of which cannot be limited as required by Protocol I. Whatever the exact meaning of this stipulation, it covers at least a reference to the principle of proportionality as contained in Art. 51 (5) (b). When using blind weapons or blind methods of combat at sea a belligerent can never say whether his warfare may be expected to cause incidental loss of civilian life, injury to civilians, damage to civilian objects, or a combination thereof, which would be excessive in relation to the concrete and direct military advantage anticipated. For mine warfare at sea the new principle of doubt in Art. 52 (3) will be of particular importance. In case of doubt, whether a merchant vessel under a neutral flag or neutral goods aboard an enemy merchant

---

[515] The legal problems are the same as in the case of the use of land mines, see, *Rauch* (note 274), 272—278.

[516] See, *supra*, 67—71.

ship, which are normally dedicated to civilian purposes, are being used to make an effective contribution to military action, they shall be presumed not to be so used. Mine warfare as a naval operation in the traditional way simply does not square with the new rules of combat, enunciated in Protocol I. Sea mines are blind weapons as long as they are not closely surveilled. Remote control may be a feasible means to adapt — to a certain degree at least — modern mine warfare to the requirements of the new humanitarian law applicable in armed conflicts. Nevertheless, naval staffs might be faced with unsurmountable difficulties to chart any effective mine warfare compatible with Protocol I.

c) Atomic Mines

The deployment of moored nuclear mines is prohibited by the 1971 Sea-Bed Treaty.[517] Free floating nuclear demolition devices are neither "emplanted" nor "emplaced" within the meaning of that treaty and, therefore, not *per se* prohibited. Their use, however, must not violate the prohibitions and restrictions of Protocol I. And in this context it is not the prohibition of indiscriminate attacks, which forecloses the use of nuclear mines in the first place. The biggest obstacle to any use of atomic demolition devices at sea in a future conflict will be created by the new rules on the protection of the natural environment. Depending upon the extent of radioactive pollution, nuclear mines will most probably in all cases cause widespread, long-term and severe damage to the marine environment and are consequently forbidden. These implications of Protocol I will be analysed in more detail later.[518]

---

517 Doc. CCD/PV. 440, 9; Doc. CCD/PV 444, 44; *Rüdiger Wolfrum*, Restricting the Use of the Sea to Peaceful Purposes: Demilitarization in Being?, in: GYIL vol. 24 (1981), 200—241 (223).

518 See, *infra*, Chapter XII.

X. Other Measures against Maritime Commerce

For completeness sake some other measures against the seaborne commerce of the enemy might be mentioned in view of the new rules in Protocol I.

1. Capture and Destruction of Enemy Property

All vessels operating under an enemy flag and all aircraft bearing enemy markings possess enemy character. However, the fact that a merchant vessel flies a neutral flag or that an aircraft bears neutral markings does not necessarily establish neutral character. Any merchant vessel or aircraft, owned or controlled by or for an enemy State, enemy persons, or any enemy corporation possesses enemy character regardless of whether or not such a vessel or aircraft operates under a neutral flag or bears neutral markings. Enemy vessels and aircraft which have been captured may, in case of military necessity, be destroyed by the capturing officer when they cannot be sent or escorted in for adjudication. The character of goods found on board a merchant vessel or aircraft is enemy if the commercial domicile of the owner is in territory belonging to or occupied by an enemy belligerent. All goods found on board enemy vessels or aircraft are presumed to be of enemy character in the absence of proof of their neutral character. Notwithstanding any transfer in title to enemy goods already at sea, these goods retain their enemy character. Goods possessing enemy character may be captured.[519]

These rules have been changed by Protocol I. Merchant ships with enemy character have to be allowed to continue their voyage to the port of destination if their cargo consists of objects indispensable for the survival of the civilian population of the enemy, in particular foodstuffs and — under adverse climatic conditions — clothing, fuel, shelter *etc.* Neither the ship, nor the cargo may be destroyed, removed or otherwise rendered useless for the sustenance of the population in need of them.[520]

---

519 Declaration of London (note 8), Arts. 55—60; US LNW (note 54), Nos. 501, 503, 633; USSR NILM (note 54), 449—450; *Perels* (note 269), 187—198; *Colombos,* Law of Prize (note 314), 67—120; *idem,* Law of the Sea (note 314), 688—729; *Herbert Arthur Smith,* The Law and Custom of the Sea, 3rd ed., London 1959, 157; *Tucker* (note 314), 74—108; see also, *Ondolf Rojahn,* article "Ships, Visit and Search", in: *Bernhardt* (note 25) vol. 4, 224—226.

520 Art. 54 par. 2.

2. Right of Angary

The right of angary is the right of a belligerent to requisition neutral merchant ships and other goods of neutrals found within its territory or territory of which it is in military occupation. However, under customary international law there are three prerequisites that have to be met. First, the vessel or goods in question must be urgently required in a case of national emergency. Secondly, full indemnification has to be paid. Thirdly, the seized vessel must be useful for the belligerent without the services of the crew, because the modern *ius angariae* does not empower the party to a conflict to compel the foreign crews to render service on the requisitioned ships. It is a controversial question whether it is justified to consider the right of angary as also being a right of neutral States. Extensive State practice during both World Wars seems to corroborate such an interpretation of the law.[521]

Under Protocol I several questions arise. Art. 54 par. 1 prohibits starvation of civilians "as a method of warfare". The exercise of the right of angary in order to overcome a national emergency is normally not such a "method" and thus cannot run afoul of this prohibition. As far as Art. 54 par. 2 is concerned we are faced with the confusing interplay of purpose and motive with respect to the destruction, removal *etc.* of goods indispensable to the survival of the civilian population, which has been already mentioned.[522] This prohibition applies only, if such indispensable objects are destroyed, removed or rendered useless for the specific purpose of denying them for their sustenance value to the civilian population or to the adverse party, whatever the motive. Since the right of angary can be exercised only for the purpose of tackling a case of national emergency, at first sight there seems to be assured that there is no incompatibility between the protection of indispensable objects and the right of angary. But this impression might prove wrong, in particular in cases where the belligerent has a choice between several neutral merchant ships, of which only one carries foodstuffs or other indispensable objects. An emerging pattern of requisitioning precisely neutral merchant vessels with foodstuffs earmarked for the enemy's civilian population would amount to a dual purpose exercise of the right of angary, *i. e.* for the purpose of dealing with a national emergency and of denying such objects for their sustenance value to the civilian

---

521 *Rainer Lagoni*, article "Angary, Right of", in: *Bernhardt* (note 25) vol. 3, 18—39; *C. L. Bullock*, Angary, in: BYIL vol. 3 (1922—23), 99—129; *Hersch Lauterpacht*, Angary and Requisition of neutral property, in: BYIL vol. 27 (1950), 455—459; *Tucker* (note 314), 348, 349; *Perels* (note 314), 221—222; *Colombos*, Law of Prize (note 314), 314—339; *Anthon-Heinrich Schröder*, Das Angarienrecht. Die Beschlagnahme von Handelsschiffen im Kriege, Hamburg 1965.

522 See, *supra*, 99—100.

population or to the adverse party. Such dual purpose angary would be a violation of Art. 54 par. 2 and might even meet the requirements of a method of warfare within the meaning of paragraph 1 of that treaty provision.

3. Unneutral Service

The term "unneutral service" or the synonymous expression "hostile assistance" implies some voluntary act in violation of neutrality which amounts to an actual assistance of a neutral ship rendered to the enemy. There are two categories of unneutral service in customary international law which may have been affected by Protocol I: sailing on behalf of the enemy government and acceptance of a belligerent convoy. Prize courts of all belligerents during the two World Wars have condemned neutral vessels when chartered by the enemy government for the carriage of an enemy cargo, because by the nature of her employment in the voyage, the neutral ship had incorporated herself in the enemy merchant marine. Under the same philosophy the acceptance of a belligerent safeconduct or convoy was considered as equivalent to rendering hostile assistance to the enemy which exposed the ship to condemnation.[523]

Here again Art. 54 Protocol I caused considerable changes. The maritime transport of objects indispensable to the survival of the civilian population of the enemy and the acceptance of a convoy for such transports can no longer be considered as hostile assistance or unneutral service. Whether executed on charter by the enemy government or undertaken unsolicited because of humanitarian reasons such service must not be regarded as interference in the armed conflict or as an unfriendly act.

---

[523] *Tucker* (note 314), 319—331; *Colombos*, Law of Prize (note 314), 231—245; *idem*, Law of the Sea (note 314), 635—648; US LNW (note 54), No. 501 and note 6 for Chapter 5.

XI. Immunity of Ships, Aircraft and other Vessels

The law of naval warfare accords to some ships, aircraft and other vessels exemption from seizure, capture, destruction or placing in prize because of considerations of humanity.

1. Legal Regime

The Hague Convention No. XI of 18 October 1907 concerning certain Restrictions with Regard to the Exercise of the Right of Capture in Naval War[524] exempts small coastal fishing vessels and small boats engaged in local coastal trade,[525] and vessels charged with religious, scientific or philanthropic missions.[526] Cartel vessels and aircraft, *i. e.* vessels and aircraft engaged in carrying out the terms of an agreement between belligerents, notably when engaged in the exchange of prisoners of war, are inviolable.[527]

The Convention for the Protection of Cultural Property in the Event of Armed Conflicts of 14 May 1954[528] grants immunity to all means of transport exclusively engaged in the transfer of cultural property.[529]

Hospital ships were for the first time accorded exemption from attack and capture by the Hague Convention of 29 July 1899 for the Adaptation to Maritime Warfare of the Principles of the Geneva Convention of 22 August 1864 which was later replaced by the Hague Convention No. X of 18 October 1907 for the Adaptation to Maritime Warfare of the Principles of the Geneva Convention.[530] This Convention was in turn superseded by the Geneva Convention for the Amelioration of the Condition of the Wounded, Sick and Shipwrecked Members of the Armed Forces at Sea of 12 August 1949.[531] The Geneva Convention of 1949 protects three types of hospital ships. First and foremost are military hospital

524 *Hinz/Rauch* (note 1), No. 1530.

525 Art. 3.

526 Art. 4.

527 US LNW (note 54), No. 503 par. 3; *Tucker* (note 314), 98.

528 *Hinz/Rauch* (note 1), No. 1510; BGBl 1967 II, 1233.

529 Art. 14.

530 *Scott* (note 83) vol. I, Oxford 1920, 650—655.

531 *Hinz/Rauch* (note 1), No. 1545.

ships, which may in no circumstances be attacked and captured, but shall at all times be respected and protected, on condition that their names and descriptions have been notified to the Parties to the conflict ten days before those ships are employed.[532] The same immunity is granted to hospital ships utilized by national Red-Cross-Societies, by officially recognized relief societies or by private persons of Parties to the conflict, and to small craft employed by the State or by the officially recognized lifeboat institutions for coastal rescue operations, it the Party to the conflict on which they depend has given them an official commission and the notification requirement has been complied with.[533] The protection of such coastal rescue craft, however, is subject to operational requirements of the naval forces.[534] Hospital ships utilized by national Red-Cross-Societies, officially recognized relief societies or private persons of neutral countries enjoy the same protection as military hospital ships and are exempt from capture, on condition that they have placed themselves under the control of one of the belligerents with the previous consent of their own governments and with the authorization of the other party to the conflict and provided further that the notification requirement has been met.[535] As far as medical aircraft are concerned, they enjoy immunity from attack in the airspace over the high seas, their own territorial sea and land territory, or in the airspace over the territorial sea and land territory of neutral countries only while flying at heights, at times and on routes specifically agreed upon between the belligerents or the belligerents and the neutral power concerned.[536]

2. Protocol I

The improvements brought about by Protocol I are considerable.

a) Ships and Vessels

Aside from the fact that Protocol I includes civilians in the term "wounded", "sick" and "shipwrecked"[537] and provides for the possibility that ships accorded immunity under the Second 1949 Geneva Convention may also carry such civilians[538] this treaty instrument of 1977 develops the above Geneva Convention in two respects. The possibility of making

---

532 Art. 22.
533 Arts. 24, 27.
534 Art. 27.
535 Art. 25.
536 Art. 39, 40.
537 Art. 8 (a), (b).
538 Art. 22 par. 1.

hospital ships available to the belligerents is now extended to the neutral State itself and to impartial international humanitarian organizations[539] and relinquishes the notification requirements for small coastal rescue craft.[540]

Protocol I, furthermore, accords to all other medical ships and craft humanitarian protection. The restrictive conditions set forth in the Geneva Convention are relaxed, the other side of the coin being, however, that the protection is rather limited. There is no notification necessary, the marking requirements are not obligatory and such ships and craft may be also used only temporarily for medical purposes.[541] These ships and craft remain subject to the laws of war. Any warship on the surface able immediately to enforce its command may order them to stop, order them off, or make them take a certain course, and they shall obey every such command. Such ships and craft may not in any other way be diverted from their medical mission so long as they are needed for the wounded, sick, and shipwrecked on board.[542] It has to be underscored that Protocol I does not contain a prohibition of capture of such vessels and craft.

b) Medical Aircraft

The legal regime of protection of medical aircraft in Protocol I is one of the outstanding achievements of the CDDH. The Protocol distinguishes four areas of operations for such aircraft:

1. Areas not controlled by an adverse party. This includes land areas physically controlled by friendly forces and internal waters,[543] the territorial sea,[544] archipelagic waters[545] and the exclusive economic zone[546] of the belligerents and areas of the high seas[547] as long as all these areas are not physically controlled by the enemy. In this area the respect and protection of medical aircraft is not dependent on any agreement with the enemy.[548]

2. Contact or similar zones. This term is restricted to land areas.[549]

---

[539] Art. 22 par. 2.

[540] Art. 22 par. 3.

[541] Art. 23.

[542] Art. 23 par. 2.

[543] Arts. 8, 10, 11 LOS Convention.

[544] Arts. 2, 3 LOS Convention.

[545] Art. 49 LOS Convention.

[546] Arts. 55, 57 LOS Convention.

[547] Arts. 86, 87 LOS Convention.

[548] Art. 25 Protocol I.

[549] Art. 26 par. 2 Protocol I.

3. Areas controlled by an adverse party. This includes the same sea areas mentioned in situation 1. above which are, this time, physically controlled by the enemy. Immunity in this case is dependent upon prior agreement to such flight from the competent authority of the adverse party. A medical aircraft which flies without or in deviation from the terms of, an agreement is subject to attack, but only as the last resort. The enemy has to take all other reasonable measures to safeguard its own interests before commencing with an attack against such medical aircraft.[550]

4. Neutral territory. The territory of neutral States includes internal waters, the territorial sea and its archipelagic waters, not however, its exclusive economic zone.[551] Here, too, an agreement with the neutral State is a prerequisite for immunity from attack for medical aircraft. If the aircraft flies without this consent, it is liable to attack. However, the neutral State is obliged to safeguard its interests by other ways and means in the first place; insofar the same rules as in situation 3 apply *mutatis mutandis*.[552]

---

550 Art. 27 Protocol I.

551 See, *supra*, 33—38.

552 Art. 31 Protocol I.

XII. Protection of the Marine Environment

The LOS Convention devotes a whole Part to the protection and preservation of the marine environment which proves the heightened awareness and consciousness of the world community towards these problems.[553] This Convention has struck a delicate compromise between the interests of the coastal States to protect their coasts and zones of sovereignty and of national jurisdiction on the one hand and the interest of the international community as a whole in the freedom of navigation on the other. I may refer in particular to the provisions dealing with international rules and national legislation to prevent, reduce or control pollution from land-based sources, activities on the continental shelf and on the deep sea-bed, by dumping, from vessels and through the atmosphere,[554] as well as with enforcement jurisdiction[555] and safeguards.[556]

1. Protocol I

As for the law of naval warfare new treaty law to protect the natural environment has been created by Protocol I. One of the three basic rules in Art. 35, restricting the choice of methods and means of warfare, consists of a prohibition "to employ methods or means of warfare which are intended or may be expected to cause widespread, long-term and severe damage to the natural environment". Similarly, Art. 55 provides: "Care shall be taken in warfare to protect the natural environment against widespread, long-term and severe damage. This protection includes a prohibition of the use of methods or means of warfare which are intended or may be expected to cause such damage to the natural environment and thereby to prejudice the health or survival of the population."

There is, of course, a close relationship between the term "damage" in the context of the law of naval warfare, and the term "pollution" within the meaning of the law of the sea. The latter is defined in the LOS Convention as the introduction by man, directly or indirectly, of

553 Part. XII, Arts. 192—237.

554 Arts. 207—212.

555 Arts. 213—222.

556 Arts. 223—233.

substances or energy into the marine environment, including estuaries, which results or is likely to result in such deleterious effects as harm to living resources and marine life, hazards to human health, hindrance to marine activities, including fishing and other legitimate uses of the sea, impairment of quality for use of sea water and reduction of amenities.[557] At any rate, the problem of Protocol I is not the question how to construe the term "damage"; the focal point of interest is the relationship between the two articles mentioned and the meaning of "widespread", "long-term" and "severe".

a) Relationship between Art. 35 and 55

Art. 55 appears in Part IV of Protocol I which deals with the civilian population, in particular its general protection against effects of hostilities. Before applying these rules to naval warfare we would have to answer the preliminary question in the affirmative whether Art. 49 extends their applicability to naval warfare at all. This is, undoubtedly, the case with respect to attacks against military objectives on land from the sea. In all other respects, however, it might be subject to questions whether damage to the marine environment on the high seas would in all cases affect the civilian population on land or whether these new rules do concern humanitarian protection within the meaning of Art. 49 par. 4 Protocol I. These diffculties would not arise if the legal content of Art. 55 were identical with that of Art. 35, which is not dependent upon passing through this eye of the needle applicable to all provisions of Section I of Part IV. The language "care shall be taken" in Art. 55 has a kind of procedural touch and this stipulation does not seem so clear-cut and unambiguous as the prohibition in Art. 35. Maybe, the difference is the same as between Art. 51 and Art. 57.[558] One could easily understand Art. 55 as being subordinate or supplementary to Art. 35. It is essential that the second sentence of Art. 55 does not add anything new and is in no way more comprehensive than Art. 35 par. 3, because the emphasis lies on the word "includes", indicating that it is just an example for the scope of application and not a definition or interpretation of the foregoing sentence.[559] While the final *ratio legis* of Art. 35 par. 3 may well be to protect the survival of humanity which could be at least seriously compromised if the natural environment were destroyed or severely damaged, this prohibition makes no reference to the civilian population at all. If a method or means of naval warfare may be expected to cause damage to the

---

[557] Art. 1 par. 4 LOS Convention.

[558] See, *supra*, 109—110.

[559] *Solf* (note 241), 198 seems to be of a different opinion.

environment meeting the three-pronged test it is prohibited according to Art. 35. In my opinion, Art. 55 merely emphasizes one of the many aspects of the possible consequences of marine pollution by belligerent acts of naval warfare. But this is neither a prerequisite for the obligation to take care under Art. 55 nor a constituent element of the prohibition in Art. 35 par. 3. As a matter of consequence, both treaty provisions have the same effect.

It is quite a different problem, whether Art. 55 would have to be construed in the light of Art. 49 in a manner that in naval warfare there has to be an effect on the civilian population. I believe that this question has to be answered affirmatively. And, therefore, it is important that Art. 35 par. 3 is not subject to this restriction, but does apply to all warfare, on land, at sea, in the air and in outer space.[560] This analysis squares with the Committee Report issued during the second session of the CDDH, which states that Art. 55 is directed at the protection of the natural environment and that the Committee approved here the same standard or criteria as is found in Art. 35 par. 3 with the addition of material concerning the civilian population. Because this article was inserted in the context of protection of the civilian population, the particular prohibition is linked to the survival of that population. The word "population" was used without the usual adjective "civilian" because it was thought that future survival is that of the population in general, without regard to combatant status. The term "health" was used in a broad sense in connection with survival to indicate actions which could be expected to cause such severe effects that even if the population survived, it would have serious health problems, such as congenital defects which produced deformed or degenerated persons. Temporary or short-term effects were not contemplated within the prohibition of this article.[561]

b) Meaning of "widespread", "long-term" and "severe"

Those familiar with the development of the law of war and the arms control treaties will think immediately of the very similar terms used in the Convention on the Prohibition of Military and Any Other Hostile Use of Environmental Modification Techniques, signed 18 May 1977.[562] Art. I of this Convention provides that the contracting parties undertake not to engage in military or other hostile use of environmental

---

560 The ICRC Commentary (note 221) correctly points out that Section I of Part III entitled "Methods and Means of Combat" extends its scope to military operations as a whole, carried out within the general framework of land, air or sea warfare, at 54.

561 O. R. (note 224) vol. XV, 281 at 81 and 82.

562 *Hinz/Rauch* (note 1), No. 1520; BGBl 1983 II, 125.

modification techniques having "widespread", "long-lasting" or "severe" effects as the means of destruction, damage or injury to any other State party. Fortunately, in this case we do have an authentic interpretation by the CCD which was transmitted along with the text of the Convention itself to the United Nations General Assembly for approval. It was the understanding of the CCD that for the purposes of the Convention the terms should be interpreted as follows:

— widespread: encompassing an area on the scale of several hundred square kilometers;

— long-lasting: lasting for a period of months, or approximately a season;

— severe: involving serious or significant disruption or harm to human life, natural and economic resources or other assets.

It was further understood that the interpretation set forth above was intended exclusively for this Convention and is not intended to prejudice the interpretation of the same or similar terms if used in connection with any other international agreement.[563] This last understanding was an implied reference to Art. 35 and 55 of Protocol I.[564]

To be sure, there are differences between Protocol I and the Environmental Modification Convention. Art. 35 and Art. 55 of Protocol I require the fulfillment of all three tests, which are cumulative. The Enmod Convention, on the other hand, lists all three criteria alternatively. In this sense, the requirements of Protocol I are more difficult to be met. But according to Art. I of the Enmod Convention the method of warfare has to have one of the three effects indicated. For Protocol I it suffices that all three effects stated conjuctively "may be expected", a considerable relaxation.

The preparatory work of the CDDH gives no guidance as to the interpretation of the element of scope of area affected and degree of damage. The record only states that they were extensively discussed.[565] The element of duration is explained in the Committee Report of the Second session as follows: "The time or duration required (*i. e.* long-term) was considered by some to be measured in decades. References to twenty or thirty years were made by some representatives as being a minimum. Others referred to battlefield destruction in France in the First World War as being outside the scope of the prohibition. The *Biotope* report states that acts of warfare which cause short-term damage to the natural environment, such as artillery bombardment are

---

[563] *Hinz/Rauch* (note 1), No. 1520 footnote 2.

[564] *Ibid.*

[565] O. R. (note 224) vol. XV, 268 at 27.

not intended to be prohibited by the Article and continues by stating that the period might be perhaps for ten years or more. However, it is impossible to say with certainty what period of time might be involved. It appears to be a widely shared assumption that battlefield damage incidental to conventional warfare would not normally be proscribed by this provision. What the article is primarily directed to is thus such damage as would be likely to prejudice, over a long term, the continued survival of the civilian population."[566] It is regrettable that neither the *Group Biotope* report nor the Committee itself elaborated on the different wording of Art. 35 par. 3 and Art. 55.[567]

2. Nuclear, Chemical and Biological Weapons

The use of atomic, chemical and biological weapons would probably always run afoul of Art. 35 par. 3 Protocol I. Recently a technological breakthrough has been achieved concerning so-called miniaturized nuclear warheads. Maybe such theater nuclear weapons can be used in some areas where they do not necessarily cause widespread, long-term and severe damage to the natural environment. This is in the first place a problem for land warfare and, of course, of attacks by naval forces against military objectives on land. It is not a specific problem of interest in connection with naval warfare.

For the purpose of this paper it seems useful to focus attention in the following sub-chapters on three military operations in naval warfare which are particularly doubtful from a legal point of view in future naval battle: the destruction of nuclear-powered and nuclear-armed enemy submarines at sea, the sinking of enemy supertankers and the attacks on enemy offshore oil-installations. All these actions shall be carried out with conventional weapons, thus the damage to the natural environment is caused exclusively by the object attacked and destroyed. In all three cases we assume that the submarine, the supertanker and the offshore rig are legitimate military objectives. Thus under the traditional law of naval warfare, one could be very brief, all three naval operations would be lawful.

3. Destruction of Nuclear Submarines

Information on nuclear powered and/or armed submarines is, of course, highly classified. Consequently, there is no hard evidence as to the collateral damage to the marine environment in the event that

[566] *Op. cit.*, 268, 269.

[567] Doc. CDDH/III/GT/35.

such a submarine is torpedoed and destroyed in armed conflict at sea. Data from the US nuclear submarines *Thresher* and *Scorpion*, lost at sea in 1963 and 1968 respectively and of the Soviet nuclear submarine which sank in 1968 in the Pacific and was, in 1977, raised from a depth of 5.200 m by the CIA in an operation called *Jennifer* are not available either.[568]

However, there has recently been some controversy in the scientific community of the United States which may shed some light on the problem what the destruction of an enemy nuclear submarine would do to the marine environment. It is certain, that such an act of naval warfare would cause radioactive pollution of the oceans and the only question is whether the damage caused would be widespread, long-term and severe. On 22 December 1982 the United States Navy published a Draft Environmental Impact Statement (DEIS) on the sea disposal of more than 100 obsolete nuclear submarines during the next three decades.[569] This statement has been severely criticized in an assessment published in the Oceanic Society's Scientific Committee Report, dated 13 March 1983.[570] At the outset, it cannot be underscored enough that we are talking about the disposal of defueled reactor plants, a situation which can not be compared to the destruction at sea of a belligerent submarine with an active reactor plant in an operational state on duty. Nevertheless ,the two documents mentioned are perhaps more indicative than scholarly research on the disposal of high-activity nuclear wastes in the oceans, because this research is based upon the assumption that the most probable mechanism will ultimately involve prior solidification of the accumulated waste and its subsequent emplacement in geological repositories under the deep ocean floor.[571] Again, a completely different set of circumstances.

Sea disposal sites considered by the US Navy for the scuttling of more than 100 decommissioned nuclear submarines include a lower continental rise area some 220 nautical miles east of Cape Hatteras, North Carolina, a Hatteras abyssal plain area some 280 nautical miles southeast of Cape Hatteras and a site some 160 nautical miles west of

[568] See, *Rauch* (note 36), 172—173, 216, 217, and "Vier Atom-U-Boote bisher gesunken", in: General-Anzeiger, Bonn 12 August 1983, 21.

[569] Draft Environmental Impact Statement on the Disposal of Decommissioned, Defueled Naval Submarine Reactor Plants, U.S. Navy, Office of the Chief of Naval Operations (OPNAV-22), Department of the Navy, Washington DC 20350.

[570] Final Report, Oceanic Society, Scientific Committee Report on DEIS, The Oceanic Society, Office Atlantic Coast: Stamford Marine Center, Magee Avenue, Stamford, Connecticut 06902; Office Pacific Coast: Fort Mason Center, Building E, San Francisco, California 94123.

[571] See, *e. g., M. S. Baxter,* The Disposal of High-activity Nuclear Wastes in the Oceans, in: MPB vol. 14 (1983), 126—132.

Mendocino, California. In times of armed conflict at sea it is impossible that belligerent actions against enemy submarines would be restricted to areas with such ideal conditions. Operational requirements will necessitate the destruction of such submarines wherever and whenever feasible, including the water column superjacent to the continental shelf which hosts the major biomass and hence food-source. US Navy estimates show sea disposal of all obsolete submarines would place 6 million curies of radioactivity in the marine environment. This is six times the level of radiation dumped at sea by the US between 1946 and 1970 when the United States ended ocean disposal of nuclear wastes.

Following the release of the US Navy DEIS the Oceanic Society consulted with scientists all over the United States to assess the document and its supporting oceanic studies and set up the Scientific Committee to review this information. Members of this Committee found the strongest arguments against sea disposal include:

— irretrievability of the submarines from the ocean floor, making it impossible to remove the subs should these ships become a significant source of radioactivity in the marine environment. The importance of being able to retrieve the submarines is increased by the limited amount of knowledge available on deep sea ecosystems;

— inadequacy of the proposed monitoring program to gauge releases of radioactivity from the submarine over extended periods of time;

— inadequacy of considerations of "worst case transportation accidents". The DEIS must be revised to reflect the statistical probability that at least one submarine will be lost on the continental shelf while being towed to a disposal site.

The principal source of concern is radioactivity which, during the operation of the submarine's propulsion system accumulates in the stainless steel equipment which comprise the vessel's reactor and steam generator. This machinery is located in a section of the sub called the reactor compartment which extends between two watertight bulkheads in the center of the submarine. 99.9 % of the 62.000 curies of radioactive materials remaining in each defueled submarine is an integral part of the corrosion-resistant alloy forming the plant components. The US scientists accuse the DEIS of not having considered and adequately assessed significant information found in the large body of scientific literature which concerns migration of radionuclides from wastes to the water column, sediments and organisms and biological pathways through which radioactivity could potentially affect human health or damage the marine environment.

According to the US Oceanic Society's Scientific Committee, experience with radioactive waste dumpsites, oil platforms and ship sunk at sea has established that any structure placed on the continental shelf attracts and holds new and more abundant communities of fishes and invertebrates. The processes at work in this phenomenon, commonly called the *artificial reef effect* are enhanced food supply in the form of fouling organisms and algae that grow on the new hard substrate. The potential for an artificial reef effect in the deep ocean presents unanswered ecological questions. The possible occurance of this phenomenon and its role as a biological pathway must be considered. In particular, the potential impact of accidental sinking of a submarine on the continental shelf receives inadequate consideration in the DEIS. Impacts of a worst case accident on the continental shelf, according to the scientists, merit additional consideration, especially in terms of predicting human health effects and the accident impact on commercial and recreational fishing as well as coastal tourism.

A fundamental concern of the Scientific Committee of the Oceanic Society centered on the absence of detailed knowledge about many aspects of deep sea ecology. Compared to other ocean ecosystems, the deep sea is poorly studied. Additional research is needed to understand the deep ocean environment and provide an adequate basis for assessing the potential impact of sea disposal of nuclear submarines.

Based upon the Scientific Committee's deliberations, the Oceanic Society opposed sea disposal of the submarines. It calls for a detailed examination of a land disposal alternative in an arid or semi-arid environment. A member of the US Council on Economic Priorities issued a paper at the same time the Oceanic Society's Scientific Committee's report was published. It disputed the Navy calculations on the amount of radioactivity in the submarines. This paper projects levels of Cobalt-60 and of Niobium-94 will be significantly higher than shown in the Navy DEIS. Based on this the paper concludes the submarines should be placed in protective storage for up to 50 years while short-lived radionuclides decay. Then, the reactor vessel should be removed and placed in a deep-mined repository (so-called "deep burial" option).[572]

The evidence available is inconclusive for our problem. There are not the faintest indications how many billions curies of radioactivity would be released into the marine environment in the event that the nuclear compartment of a Soviet *Taifun* class or US *Trident* class submarine, each with almost 30 000 tons deadweight, would be hit by a missile or a torpedo. If scientists raise serious questions as to the

[572] See, Editor's Note on page 21 of the Final Report (note 427).

safety and wisdom of sinking outdated and defueled nuclear submarines in the ocean I have not the slightest doubt that the scholars who evaluated and criticized the US Navy DEIS would unanimously reach the conclusion that this was an act of warfare which may be expected to cause widespread, long-term and severe damage to the natural environment.

4. Torpedoing of Supertankers

It is not difficult to imagine what would happen to the marine environment if a supertanker of the enemy were torpedoed after the numerous disasters involving oil tankers, among which the *Torrey Canyon*, the *Argo Merchant* and the *Amoco Cadiz* are the most famous.

On 18 March 1967, the tanker *Torrey Canyon*, carrying 119.000 metric tons of light Arabian crude from Kuwait grounded near the Scilly islands off the coast of southwest England. 14.000 tons of oil were swept ashore on the rocks of Cornwall. 20.000 tons crossed the Channel and reached the coast of Brittany. 50.000 tons were driven by northeasterly winds into the Gulf of Biscay. 15.000 tons evaporated in the air, the rest of roughly 20.000 tons caught fire when the wreck was intentionally destroyed with explosives.[573]

On 15 December 1976, the tanker *Argo Merchant* carrying 28.000 metric tons of so-called No. 6 fuel oil ran aground on Fishing Rip of Nantucket Shoals and soon began to leak her cargo into the surrounding waters. Later, she broke into three parts which eventually sank, the bow section having floated off the original wreck site 2,8 km southeast of the stern and midsection. A scientific survey of the wreck site, conducted in February 1977 indicated sediment contamination in a 10—15 km² area.[574]

On 16 March 1978, the Liberian-registered tanker *Amoco Cadiz*, carrying 120.000 tons of light Iranian crude oil and 100.000 tons of light Arabian crude as well as 4000 tons of her own fuel (Bunker C) was grounded on the coast of Brittany. The tanker, 233.680 tons deadweight, had suffered steering failure some 13 km north of the Ile d'Ouessant. Despite the assistance of an ocean-going German salvage tug and with severe difficulties caused by high winds — force 8, gusting to 9 and 10

[573] Umweltprobleme der Nordsee, Sondergutachten Juni 1980 des Rates von Sachverständigen für Umweltfragen, errichtet am 28. Dezember 1971 durch das Bundesinnenministerium, 223—225; *James Eric Smith* (ed.), Torrey Canyon Pollution and Marine Life, Plymouth 1968.

[574] *Eva J. Hoffmann/James G. Quinn*, Gas Chromatographic Analysis of Argo Merchant Oil and Sediment Hydrocarbons at the Wreck Site, in: MPB vol. 10 (1979), 20—24.

on the Beaufort scale — and the heavy swell, the tanker was driven ashore making this the largest oil spillage ever recorded. Some 6 minutes later her engine room was flooded, electricity supporting ceased and radio contact was lost. In the early hours the following morning, the crew was evacuated by helicopter. As the tide ebbed the *Amoco Cadiz* broke in two immediately forward of the bridge, breaking 4 of her 12 cargo tanks and releasing about 50.000 tons of crude oil during the following day. The oil was driven ashore and the coastline of about 5 km became heavily polluted. During the 18th of March the oil slick spread to cover an area about 40 km long and 10 km wide; and cargo loss had risen to 80.000 tons. On Sunday, 19 March, the slick was reported as being 100 km long and 10 km wide. Along the coast, pollution extended from Pointe de St. Mathieu west of Brest to the Ile Vièrge near Aber-Wrac'. Over the next days the oil continued to move slowly eastwards. By 24 March rising winds and heavy seas caused the *Amoco Cadiz* to break up further, releasing most if not all of her cargo. It was estimated that only about 35.000 tons remained in the wreck. On 25 March the main oil slick was almost stationary, and extended out from the shore to a distance of 2 km, with a band of thinner oil 6 km seaward of it. The length of coast more or less polluted was around 200 km, which later extended to about 300 km. Some 64.000 tons of oil went ashore during the first two weeks and after a month of clean-up activities and natural erosion only 11.000 tons remained on the beaches. Large amounts of oil was deposited and some stranded oil remained buried in the sand of beaches.[575]

There is no doubt in my mind that in all three cases the damage to the marine environment was "widespread" within the meaning of Protocol I. The more difficult questions are connected with the element of duration and the degree of intensity of the damage.

It is difficult to give a complete record of the severity of the damage to the marine environment by the sinking of an oil tanker. Much depends upon the proportion of volatile fractions in the crude oil which can be expected to evaporate soon after discharge and upon prevailling meteorological and oceanographic conditions.[576] And there still seems to be scant knowledge about the long-term ramifications of a major oil spill. The provisional assessment of the impact of the *Amoco Cadiz* oil after 6 months showed that about 30 % of the fauna and less than 5 % of the flora was destroyed locally. Some fish showed pathological

---

[575] *A. J. O'Sullivan*, The Amoco Cadiz Oil Spill, in: MPB vol. 9 (1978), 123—125; *Lucien Laubier*, The Amoco Cadiz Oil Spill — Lines of Study and early Observations, *op. cit.*, 285—287.

[576] *O'Sullivan* (note 575), 126.

changes and the local sediments remained contaminated. There had been none of the dramatic botanical changes reported on the Cornish coast following the use of more toxic dispersants after the *Torrey Canyon* disaster. The moderate nature of the damage was attributed to the turbulence of the local sea which dispersed the oil and in the first place by the limited use of highly toxic dispersants which destroyed almost the entire fauna on the coast of Cornwall.[577]

Since the oceanographic community had been taken by surprise in the case of the *Torrey Canyon* attention should focus on the more detailed investigations after the *Amoco Cadiz* wreck which was the most spectacular and potentially most damaging marine pollution event in the history of oil pollution. But it seems too early to render a final judgment with respect to the long-term repercussions and the severeness of the environmental damage of this oil spill. The oceanographic and biological consequences will be recorded, analyzed and perhaps argued until the end of this decade according to the editors of the *Marine Pollution Bulletin* which devoted the entire November 1978 issue to a number of reports about studies already completed 20 months after this incident and which permitted some interim descriptions and assessments.[578] According to these accounts about 40 % of the oil was probably lost to the air where photodegradation could take place. Onshore winds in the first days caused nauseating smells but there was no evidence of the postulated possible widespread damage to crops or livestock. Immediate toxic effects from Arabian crude was not particularly high but the naphthenes in the Iranian crude added a lesser known hazard. The rapid natural dispersal to depth of light oil in rough seas was clearly demonstrated, with local damage to mid-water and bottom fauna. Potential damage to more distant fisheries and beaches seems to have been reduced or prevented by dilution resulting from a combination of mainly natural dispersal. Much finely divided oil was rapidly sedimented to the bottom and transported with silt. The duration of its effect in fine sediments has yet to be determined. Some toxic effects of these oils were seen on shore even after oil had travelled 90 km or more in about 5 days.[579]

Some general conclusions were offered by *M. Lucien Laubier* from the *Centre Oceanologique de Bretagne:*

1. The fresh crude oil was rapidly dispersed by very rough seas during the first two weeks and caused the death of an impressive

[577] Umweltprobleme der Nordsee, Sondergutachten (note 573), 225; *W. R. P. Bourne,* The Impact of the Amoco Cadiz, in: MPB vol. 10 (1979), 216.

[578] Vol. 9 (1978), No. 11 (281—311).

[579] *Molly F. Spooner,* Editorial Introduction, MPB vol. 9 (1978), 281—284.

number of marine invertebrates and fishes. This period of heavy mortality in the intertidal and shallow subtidal environment apparently ceased rapidly at the beginning of April.

2. The general spreading of the pollution was essentially wind-controlled.

3. On the beaches, the phenomenon of spring sand accretion in the upper part of beaches with high tidal coefficient buried the heavy oil deposits within the sand, down to depth of 80 cm.

4. A large amount of oil spread into the *Abers* — submerged estuaries of small rivers about 10 to 15 km long and no more than 1 km wide with sandy and muddy areas — and the oil will remain for long in these protected, low energy areas. It seems that in the muddy sediments the oil sunk into the sediment through the numerous galleries and holes resulting from biological activity.

5. The total hydrocarbon content of the subtidal sediment in the Bay of Lannion and the Bay of Morlaix varied from 1—2 % from 8 m down to 30 m depth. This heavy pollution gives a hypothetical figure of some 40.000 tons of oil in the subtidal sediment. Density of populations of amphipods were reduced to one tenth of their usual values.

6. The bird population had been directly affected by the oil with more than 4.500 dead birds being collected.

7. At a distance off the coast of at least 4 nautical miles the quantitative hauls of zooplancton and fish larvae did not reveal significant differences between polluted and non-polluted areas. The commercial fishing activity in the area started again after one month interruption.

8. The oyster beds within the *Abers* were highly polluted and the remaining oysters were contaminated at a level of 150—400 ppm in total hydrocarbons.[580]

As far as the element of duration of the environmental damage is concerned sediment contamination seems to be the most important consequence. Hydrocarbon analysis of oiled sandy beach samples indicate that large amounts of stranded sheen oil and mousse can be accommodated in sandy shorelines. Preliminary estimates suggest that up to 7,5 kg of oil may be accommodated under one square meter of sandy beach, and that as much as 900 metric tons or 4.800 barrels of *Amoco Cadiz* cargo lies buried within sandy sediments. Such buried

---

[580] *Laubier* (note 575), 285—287; *C. Chasse,* The Ecological Impact on and near Shores by the Amoco Cadiz Oil Spill, in: MPB vol. 9 (1978), 298—301; *P. Hope Jones et al.,* Birds oiled during the Amoco Cadiz Incident — an Interim Report, *op. cit.,* 307—310.

oil will become available for re-entry into the marine environment during the winter beach erosional phases. Acute lethal toxicity of freshly stranded *Amoco Cadiz* oil was determined to be intermediate to that of Bunker C and Kuwait crude oil. Simulated weathering studies suggest that this acute toxicity will increase directly with weathering.[581]

5. Attacks on Off-Shore Oil Installations

Unfortunately, the world knows already a massive oil spill as a by-product of an armed conflict — the almost 3 years old Iran—Iraq war. Since only few scientific data are available on the slick that covers thousands of square miles of the Persian Gulf and threatens major economic and environmental damage to riparian States, it seems appropriate to mention some other similar incidents whose repercussions would seem to be identical if they were caused by belligerent action.

On 22 April 1977 a blow-out occurred during maintenance operations on the *Bravo* platform of the North Sea *Ekofisk* oil field and oil began to escape at a rate of 2000 to 3000 tons a day. The well was capped on 30 April 1978. It is estimated that altogether 20.000—30.000 tons of oil escaped into the North Sea. According to the Institute of Continental Shelf Surveys roughly 40 % of the oil evaporated due to the high temperature of 75 centigrade. On the surface the slick formed stripes 1—2 km long and 10 m wide, which covered an area of 3.000 km^2. The meteorological conditions were so advantageous that no coast was polluted.[582] Analyses of samples collected during and following the blow-out showed the presence of petroleum hydrocarbons from the blow-out in some of the water samples, but fish and sediments, collected up to a week after it began showed no evidence of a contribution from the oil spill.[583]

On 3 June 1979 the *Ixtoc I* well in the Bay of Campeche, Mexico blew out and caught fire. The well continued to spew oil for almost eight months, eventually releasing an estimated 450.000 tons of oil.

---

[581] *J. H. Vandermeulen et al.*, Sediment Penetration of Amoco Cadiz Oil, Potential for Future Release and Toxicity, in: MPB vol. 10 (1979), 222—224; *Louis Cabioch et al.*, Preliminary Observations on Pollution of the Sea Bed and Disturbance of Sub-Littoral Communities in Northern Brittany by Oil from the Amoco Cadiz, *op. cit.*, 303—307; also the Sondergutachten Umweltprobleme der Nordsee (note 573) arrives at the conclusion that the contamination of sediments is the long-term pollution problem after the Amoco Cadiz Oil Spill, at 228.

[582] Umweltprobleme der Nordsee, Sondergutachten (note 573), 222—223.

[583] *R. J. Law*, Determination of Petroleum Hydrocarbons in Water, Fish and Sediments Following the Ekofisk Blow-Out, in: MPB vol. 9 (1978), 321—324; see also, *Robert T. Bassett*, Small Oil Spill kills 10—20.000 Seabirds in North Norway, in: MPB vol. 10 (1979), 253—255; see also, the Editorial "Ecofiasco", in: MPB vol. 8 (1977), 121—122.

It was the largest oil spill in the history of offshore oil operations and immediately considered as an ecological disaster. The pollution of the marine environment extended to the beaches of southern Texas. By 12 June a slick 180 km long and 80 km wide had already formed.[584] The weathering of the *Ixtoc I* crude oil was high. *Petroleum Mexicano* initially claimed that 30 % was being lost by evaporation.[585] Some scientists estimated that in eight weeks 60 % or more of the hydrocarbons was lost.[586]

Several studies had been conducted in the Campeche Bank area prior to the *Ixtoc I* blow-out.[587] With the results of these studies as a baseline an interdisciplinary study of the area was performed in March 1980 in order to evaluate the effects of the blow-out. The direct result of any oil spill in the marine environment is the dissolution of a portion of that oil into marine waters. This soluble fraction has been shown to be toxic to marine plants and animals.[588] The toxicity of oil accommodated seawater from the oil slick has been reported to be low for certain marine invertebrates. However, water-soluble component's toxicities and long-term effects vary with the organism being exposed and length of exposure. The scope and long-term effects of the oil accommodated seawater from *Ixtoc I* have yet to be determined. Preliminary findings indicated that the dispersal in a large reservoir such as the Mexican Gulf does not readily occur in the immediate area of an oil slick. It appears that large volumes of oil-contaminated seawater are able to remain in patches which are chemically distinct from surrounding waters.[589]

Details of the ecological disaster in the Persian Gulf are not known, because no independent experts are permitted to visit the leaking oil wells in the *Nowruz* field off the coast of Iran. It apparently began in January 1983 when a damaged Iranian rig, shut down in 1981 started to leak. The Iranians tried to cap the well but Iraqi helicopters routed the repair party. In one of the helicopter attacks three platforms were

---

[584] Mexican Offshore Blow-Out Rivals Ekofisk, in: MPB vol. 10 (1979), 215—216; *M. L. Lizarraga-Partida et al.*, Effects of the Ixtoc I Blow-Out on Heterotrophic Bacteria, in: MPB vol. 13 (1982), 67; *S. A. Macko et al.*, Gulf of Mexico Dissolved Hydrocarbons Associated with the Ixtoc I Mousse, in: MPB vol. 13 (1982), 174—177.

[585] Mexican Offshore Blow-Out Rivals Ekofisk (note 584), 215.

[586] *Lizarraga-Partida et al.* (note 584), 70.

[587] *A. V. Botello et al.*, Baseline studies for hydrocarbons and organic carbon isotope ratios of recent sediments in the Bank of Campeche before the Ixtoc I oilspill, in: Second Chemical Congress of the North American Continent, American Chemical Society, Las Vegas, Nevada, 24—29 August 1980.

[588] *Macko et al.* (note 584), 174.

[589] *Op. cit.*, 175.

destroyed or severely damaged, and two of them set afire. The ongoing war is preventing experts from capping the wells. The coasts of Kuwait, Bahrain, Saudi-Arabia, Katar, the United Arab Emirates and of both belligerents are threatened. A meeting of the officials of eight Gulf States took place in April in Kuwait, but negotiations quickly fell into deadlock. Since the oil spill was first spotted in March 1983 in a weather-satellite photograph the slick has flattened out and broken up in heavy seas and strong southeasterly winds. As the lighter parts of the heavy crude evaporate the rest forms large tarry blobs that tend to float about three feet below the surface. Oil experts estimate that 5.000 barrels of oil a day are lost from the cracked underwater wells in the *Nowruz* field and by now the disaster can be compared to the *Amoco Cadiz* accident or the *Ixtoc I* blow-out. Some experts predict the slick may pass out into the open sea through the Strait of Hormuz. The countries along the Gulf coast are preparing for the worst if the oil invades their huge desalination plants which provide drinking waters. Specialists would need at least four weeks to cap all three wells. Due to the delicate ecosystem in the Persian Gulf, an enclosed or semi-enclosed sea with an average depth of only 25 meters, the existing slick could stay very long. Panic buying in Quatar sent the price of a barrel of mineral water up from 32 Dollars to 145 Dollars until the government stepped in to stop hoarding.[590]

In all three cases — *Ecofisk, Ixtoc I* and *Nowruz* — little divergence of view seems to be possible with respect to the scope of area affected as meeting the requirement of "widespread" within the meaning of Art. 35 par. 3 Protocol I. As for the degree of damage and the element of duration much would depend on a more thorough investigation of the biological and oceanographic implications of oil-spills of that magnitude. The legal advisers of naval staffs have to rely on the expertise of scholars in the field of natural science. It can only be hoped that the responsible naval planners of the major maritime powers order such investigations before revising their Manuals of Naval Warfare. The lawyer may only emphasize again that Art. 35 par. 3 (and Art. 55 par. 1) of Protocol I does not prohibit methods and means of warfare which "cause" widespread, long-term and severe damage to the marine environment, but which "may be expected to cause" such damage thus injecting an element of objective expectation which suffices to render such methods and means of naval warfare unlawful.

[590] Der Spiegel, Nr. 23/1983, 106—112, "Ach ja, der Ölteppich, schlimm, schlimm"; Newsweek, April 18, 1983, 19, "A Massive Oil Slick Plagues the Gulf".

XIII. Reprisals

At the beginning of this chapter I should underline that the problem will not be tackled whether one can retaliate against neutrals, who have never injured the belligerent and never violated the laws of neutrality. This problem, peculiar to the exercise of reprisals in naval warfare, cannot be discussed here, since it is not influenced by Protocol I or the LOS Convention.

Insofar as measures are justified as reprisals there is always an admission involved that these measures are in fact illegal, since the doctrine of reprisals presupposes that a violation of international law is being countered by a breach of the rules and customs of war. In both World Wars we have seen an unsurpassed escalation of reprisals and counter-reprisals, which makes it extremely difficult to render a judgment on the legality of the acts of naval warfare in question.

1. Legal Regime

Belligerent reprisals are acts, otherwise illegal, which are exceptionally permitted to a belligerent as a reaction against illegal acts of warfare committed by an enemy. The purpose of reprisals is to induce compliance with the laws of war by the other party to the conflict. Reprisal is distinguished from retortion in that a reprisal is a retaliation against an illegal act and has the legal character of an enforcement action which may involve the use of armed force. In other words, reprisals are never to be taken merely for revenge, but only as a last resort to induce an enemy to desist from unlawful practices. The acts resorted to by way of reprisal need not conform to those complained of by the injured belligerent, but should not be disproportionate.[591]

2. State Practice

a) World War I

The starting point for the escalation of reprisals and counter-reprisals between 1914 and 1918 was the refusal of the Entente Powers on 22 August 1914 to abide by the Declaration of London as suggested by

[591] US LNW (note 54), No. 310.

the government of the United States,[592] the extension of the doctrine of continuous voyage to the carriage of all contraband by the British Order in Council of 29 October 1914[593] and the establishment of the British War Zone on 3 November 1914.[594] These three measures were considered by the Entente Powers as lawful modifications and additions to the traditional rules of naval warfare which they judged indispensable to the efficient conduct of their naval operations.[595] Or to couch it in the terms of the British War Zone Decree of 3 November 1914, they were considered as "exceptional measures appropriate to the novel conditions under which this war is being carried on".[596] The Central Powers were of a completely different point of view. In their opinion the Entente measures were blatant violations of the rules of naval warfare which could be lawfully answered by reprisals.

Thus Germany, on 4 February 1915, proclaimed a War Zone of her own by way of retaliation for various violations of international law by the Entente Powers, notably the measures in respect to contraband, disregard of the Declarations of Paris and London, and the conversion of the North Sea into a war zone. A memorandum of 4 February 1915, issued by the German government, stated that the German war zone was justified as retaliatory measure, rendered necessary by various methods of the enemy to destroy the neutral trade with Germany for the purpose of reducing the civilian population to starvation, in particular by treating the whole North Sea as a military area and thereby establishing a blockade of neutral ports and coasts.[597]

One month later the Entente Powers retaliated against this reprisal with the Anglo-French blockade of Germany. The British Prime Minister declared in the House of Commons that these measures had been decided upon in the exercise of an "unquestionable right of retaliation" against the German War Zone Decree of 4 February 1915, which was denounced as violating the usages of war. In the retaliatory measures "blockade", "contraband" or other legal terms did not occur, which the British Prime Minister explained in the House of Commons as follows: "... in dealing with an opponent who has openly repudiated all the restraints of law and humanity we are not going to allow our efforts to be strangled in a network of juridical meshes."[598]

---

[592] See, *supra*, 83.

[593] See, *supra*, 97, 98; *Garner* (note 320) vol. II, 295, 296.

[594] See, *supra*, 103; *Garner* (note 320) vol. I, 333, 345.

[595] See, *supra*, 84.

[596] *Garner* (note 320) vol. I, 333.

[597] *Op. cit.*, 335; see also, vol. II, 320.

[598] *Colombos*, Law of Prize (note 314), 266; *Garner* (note 320) vol. II, 321, 322, 323.

Both the German War Zone Decree of February 1915 and the Anglo-French blockade measures of March 1915 evoked strong protests from neutral countries, including the United States. In a diplomatic note of 18 February the German government defended its Decree as a measure of overpowering military necessity and a justifiable act of reprisal against Great Britain. Germany, the note said, had scrupulously observed valid international rules regarding naval warfare, put into force the Declaration of London without any alteration and observed its rules albeit some of them were diametrically opposed to the military interests of Germany. The British government, on the other hand, had not hesitated to violate the rules of the Declaration and by a procedure contrary to all humanitarian principles had cut-off all supplies to Germany, thereby endeavouring to starve the peaceful civilian population. In view of this situation the German government, according to the verbal note, saw itself compelled after six months of patient and watchful waiting to meet England's "murderous method of conducting maritime war" with drastic counter-measures.[599]

In this context again mention may be made of the sinking of the *Lusitania*.[600] On 10 May 1915, three days after the incident, the German Foreign Office in a note to the US government declared that the responsibility for the tragic deaths of civilians rested upon the British government "which through its plan of starving the civilian population of Germany has forced Germany to retaliatory measures".[601] In a diplomatic note of 28 May 1915 the German government asserted again that the destruction of the *Lusitania* was a justifiable act of reprisal against Great Britain for her "inhuman attempt to starve the civilian population of Germany by means of an unlawful blockade and an unwarranted extension of the rules relating to contraband". The drowning of a few hundred non-combatant enemy persons or even of neutrals was no greater crime than the slow starvation of a whole nation and the British government had repudiated all the rules of international law and disregarded all the rights of neutrals.[602]

On 1 February 1917 Germany promulgated the "Barred" Zone Decree which is commonly regarded as the beginning of unrestricted submarine warfare. This measure, too, was avowedly adopted in retaliation against Great Britain for "using her naval power in a criminal attempt to force Germany to submission by starvation in contempt of international law".[603]

---

[599] *Garner* (note 320) vol. II, 325.

[600] See, *supra*, 104—105.

[601] *Garner* (note 320) vol. I, 357.

[602] *Op. cit.*, 358.

[603] *Op. cit.*, 338.

On 16 February 1917 a British Order in Council decreed the capture and condemnation of all vessels carrying goods of enemy origin or destination encountered at sea on their way to or from a port in any neutral country, affording means of access to the enemy territory without calling at a British or Allied port.[604] This Order was explicitly taken as a reprisal to the German "Barred" Zone Decree of 1 February 1917.[605]

If one pays attention to the chronological order of events one has to admit that the Entente measures were taken at the beginning. And they did violate the law of nations. Consequently, the Central Powers could exercise their right of reprisal, and their pertinent countermeasures were not themselves a breach of the law of naval warfare. Since even Anglo-Saxon authors after World War I could not avoid admitting that the warfare waged by the Entente Powers on the seas did not conform to the traditional rules of naval warfare, generally recognized by all civilized nations, they resorted to a device which consisted of a distinction between "technical" and "substantial" violations of the law and usages of naval warfare. This almost seems to correspond to the differentiation between the letter and the spirit of international law. The Entente Powers, they argued, were only technically violating the law governing blockade and contraband while the Central Powers committed substantial breaches of the rules of law by their submarine warfare. Quite obviously, there are no reprisals possible against the mere technical violations of the Entente Powers, which were said to have justifiedly not applied "rigid technical standards" by adapting the "impractical" traditional law of blockade and contraband to "modern conditions". Since these acts were allegedly lawful the Central Powers could not exercise a right of reprisal. These acts of reprisal actually taken by the Central Powers were — from the Entente point of view — new gross violations of international law as interpreted and applied by them. Hence they could, in turn, again serve as justification for real counter-reprisals. As for the alleged violations "in substance" committed by the Central Powers they could, of course, be answered by reprisals and no counter-reprisals were admissible. From this cynical approach retaliatory measures as reprisals could be lawfully resorted to only by the Entente Powers.[606]

b) World War II

From a chronological point of view, the spiral of escalation again started with a British measure, *i. e.* the British contraband lists of 3 September 1939 which caused the German government to amend its

---

604 See, *supra*, 84.

605 *Colombos*, Law of Prize (note 314), 267.

606 *Op. cit.*, 269—276; see also, *Mallison* (note 400), 66, 67.

own lists likewise. These British contraband lists were considered by the Axis Powers as a first violation of the Declaration of 2 September 1939 in which the French and British governments solemnly and publicly affirmed their intentions to conduct hostilities with the firm desire of sparing the civilian population. Concerning the use of naval forces, the two governments pledged themselves strictly to the rules formulated by the Protocol of 1936.[607] The German government in a diplomatic note of 17 September 1939 addressed to the French government answered this Declaration with accusations that the British government had already flagrantly contradicted its solemn undertaking to spare the civilian population by promulgating extensive contraband lists which disregarded all recognized rules of naval warfare and thus opened the starvation blockade against women and children. The German government reserved the right to retaliate against any breach of the law on the part of its enemies and this in such a manner as might seem appropriate. With regard to the starvation blockade waged by Great Britain against women and children, they reserved the right to reply with the use of those weapons which were at the government's disposal for this purpose and which would demonstrate to the enemy the fearful consequences of the methods that he had adopted.[608]

On 6 October 1939 the British government stated to the Japanese Foreign Office that it did not intend to apply the Declaration of London in one way or another. As far as continuous voyage was concerned, the British government would apply this doctrine without any distinction between absolute and conditional contraband.[609]

Admiral Raeder in an interview with the Dutch newspaper *Allgemeenen Handelsblatt* on 19 October 1939 explained the principles of the German naval warfare as follows: "Submarine warfare will be conducted strictly according to the German Prize Ordinance of 28 August 1939 which incorporates fully the stipulations of the London Protocol of 1936 on submarine warfare. Under the recognized rules, however, submarines are entitled to break any armed resistance. It is to be feared that incidents will be created by Great Britain arming its merchant ships, in particular because British merchant ships with all probability will receive the same orders as in World War I, namely to use their weapons in violation of international law against submarines. If this should be the case, Germany would be forced to take countermeasures, because it cannot permit that the lives of submarine crews were endangered by unlawful attacks. Similarly, Germany had already been forced to adapt

[607] Urkunden zum Seekriegsrecht (note 70), No. 27.
[608] *Op. cit.*, No. 2.
[609] *Op. cit.*, No. 29.

its own contraband list to the extensive British list of 4 September 1939 and to abandon the principle contained in the German Prize Ordinance that the doctrine of continuous voyage is not to be applied to conditional contraband, because Great Britain does apply this doctrine to all contraband goods."[610]

Although all belligerents had solemnly declared to continue to respect the principles of chivalrous and humane naval warfare, the stage was set pretty soon for an all-out escalation of reprisals and counter-reprisals. On 17 August 1940 Germany declared a total blockade against Great Britain as a reprisal against British violations of the law of naval warfare. The following breaches of the law of naval warfare, among others, were mentioned: declaring all foodstuffs conditional contraband and treating them as absolute contraband, armament of British merchant vessels, in order to use them as a weapon against German U-boats, laying of drifting mines, deployment of merchant vessels for belligerent acts, use of fishery boats as submarine traps, announcement on 8 May 1940 by the British government to attack in the Skagerrak all German ships by day and all ships by night at sight without any warning whatsoever, requisitioning of the merchant navy of Norway, Denmark, the Netherlands, Belgium and France, introduction of the navicert-system *etc.* The German government announced that it would from that day on retaliate in kind and use its methods and means of warfare with the same brutality.[611] The British Ministry of Information on the same day issued a statement, rejecting all German accusations and countering with the accusation that it was Germany that violated all rules of international law while trying to blockade the British islands.[612]

3. Protocol I

The prohibition of reprisals against the persons and objects protected by the so-called "Geneva-stream" of the law of war, in particular the wounded, sick, shipwrecked, prisoners of war, civilians in occupied territory and medical and religious personnel, has been an integral part of the law of war since the four 1949 Geneva Conventions or even earlier. In so far Protocol I did not contribute much.[613] A completely new chapter of the law of conflict, however, was written by the CDDH with respect to the rules of combat constituting the so-called "Hague-stream" of the law of war. This body of law until now distinguished itself from the

[610] *Op. cit.*, No. 3; see also, the interview between *Admiral Raeder* and a correspondent of NBC New York of 4 March 1940, *op. cit.*, No. 4.

[611] *Op. cit.*, No. 286.

[612] *Op. cit.*, No. 287.

[613] See, Art. 20.

"Red-Cross-law" by accepting reprisals as an important means for inducing the observance of legitimate warfare. Protocol I has changed that dramatically.

Protocol I contains the following prohibitions of reprisals that will be of importance in future naval warfare:

— Attacks against the civilian population or civilians by way of reprisals are prohibited;[614]

— Civilian objects shall not be the object of reprisals;[615]

— It is prohibited to make cultural and spiritual objects and places of worship the object of reprisals;[616]

— Objects indispensable to the survival of the civilian population shall not be made the object of reprisals;[617]

— Attacks against the natural environment by way of reprisals are prohibited,[618] and

— It is prohibited to make dams, dykes or nuclear generating stations and other military objectives located at or in their vicinity the object of reprisals.[619]

The ramifications of these prohibitions on the law of naval warfare cannot be overestimated. Even as an act of belligerent reprisal a starvation blockade or the treatment of foodstuffs as absolute contraband would be unlawful. The torpedoing of a 500.000 tons supertanker with a cargo of crude oil close to the coast of the enemy by way of reprisal would be prohibited, if the scuttling of such a ship would constitute a violation of Art. 55 Protocol I, namely cause widespread, long-term and severe damage of the natural environment and thereby prejudice the health or survival of the population. Even if the enemy's naval forces repeatedly engage in merciless naval bombardments of military objectives on land grossly violating the principles of distinction, identification and proportionality, indiscriminate attacks by the injured belligerent as acts of reprisal remain prohibited by Protocol I.

I have never hesitated to set forth my personal opinion with respect to belligerent reprisals. Despite the experience with the spiral of escalation of reprisals and counter-reprisals in both World Wars I submit, that

[614] Art. 51 par. 6.
[615] Art. 52 par. 1.
[616] Art. 53 (c).
[617] Art. 54 par. 4.
[618] Art. 55 par. 2.
[619] Art. 56 par. 4.

reprisals are the one and most often only means to convince the enemy that he had better abide by the rules and customs of war. Apart from belligerent reprisals there are only resorts to world opinion, influence of legal advisers, possibly protecting powers, or after the war, war crimes tribunals. But these means are not going to have much impact on a belligerent who is convinced of winning the war. Therefore, we need legitimate belligerent reprisals for the vigorous enforcement of the law of war.[620]

However, there were only few objections at the CDDH. The Canadian representative pointed out that it had to be remembered that when an enemy bombed major centers of population no government would stand idly by when the only way of stopping the bombing was to do the same to the other side. His delegation did not wish an unenforceable provision to be adopted, disrespect for which would lead to disrespect for the whole Protocol.[621] The delegate of Great Britain shared the fears expressed by the Canadian representative that the prohibition on reprisals might weaken the whole Protocol.[622] The delegate of France had the same misgivings. Grave violations of Protocol I would undoubtedly provoke a reaction on the part of the victims, whose governments could hardly forbid them to take reprisals with a view to ending such violations. The prohibitions of reprisals might, in certain circumstances, favor a party which violated the Protocol and penalize a party which observed it. The pertinent draft treaty provision should, therefore, be deleted. If it were to be retained it should be amended to allow for the possibility of reprisals in the circumstances indicated but subject to three conditions. In the first place, the decision to resort to reprisals should be taken by the government alleging the violations of the Protocol, not by the military commander; secondly, the adverse party should be given advance warning that reprisals would be taken if the violation was continued or renewed; and thirdly, the reprisals should be proportionate to the violation they were designed to end.[623] Also the Australian delegation opposed the adoption of a provision which prohibited reprisals against civilian objects in all circumstances. In the view of the Australian delegation a reprisal during armed conflict would be an act by a government which would normally be a violation of international law, but which becomes permissible when carried out in response to a previous violation of international law by an adversary. A reprisal was a sanction to deter further violation of the law, and was

620 *Rauch* (note 281), 103—106; see also, Arts. 82, 83 and 90 Protocol I.

621 O. R. (note 224) vol. XIV, 55.

622 *Op. cit.*, 65 and 139.

623 *Op. cit.*, 65.

not an act of vengeance. The availability of this sanction might persuade an adversary not to commit violations of the law in the first place.[624]

I strongly believe that it is not the existence of belligerent reprisals as such that causes difficulties and leads to the above mentioned spiral of escalation. It is the uncertainty what the term means and the ambiguities connected with it, not to mention the fact that the concept of reprisal was often used as a cover-up for acts of warfare which did not intend at all to convince the adversary to stop a certain behavior or certain actions. Protocol I would have served its humanitarian intentions and purposes better by deleting all prohibitions of reprisals in the "Hague-stream" of the law of war and inserting instead a clear and unambiguous definition of the term "reprisal" as suggested by the French delegation on 22 April 1976. This draft article reads as follows:

"1. In the event that a party to a conflict commits serious, manifest and deliberate breaches of its obligations under this Protocol, and a party victimized by these breaches considers it imperative to take action to compel the Party violating its obligations to cease doing so, the victimized party shall be entitled, subject to the provisions of this article, to resort to certain measures which are designed to repress the breaches and induce compliance with the Protocol, but which would otherwise be prohibited by the Protocol.

2. The measures described in paragraph 1 of this article may be taken only when the following conditions are met:

a) The measures may be taken only when other efforts to induce the adverse party to comply with the law have failed or are not feasible, and the victimized party clearly has no other means of ending the breach;

b) The decision to have recourse to such measures must be taken at the highest level of the government of the victimized party; and

c) The party committing the breach must be given specific, formal, and prior warning that such measures will be taken if the breach is continued or renewed.

3. If it proves imperative to take these measures, their extent and their means of application shall in no case exceed the extent of the breach which they are designed to end. The measures may not involve any actions prohibited by the Geneva Conventions of 1949. The measures must cease, in all events, when they have achieved their objective, namely, cessation of the breach which prompted the measure."[625]

---

[624] *Op. cit.* vol. VI, 176.

[625] *Op. cit.*, vol. III, 324; see also, the previous French proposal of an article 74 *bis* dated 19 February 1975, *op. cit.*, 323.

XIV. Conclusion

When *Captain Alfred Thayer Mahan,* United States Navy, later an admiral and delegate to the First Hague Peace Conference in 1899, wrote his famous book, "The Influence of Sea Power upon History",[626] a decade before the turn of the century, he did not consider international law as a factor for the successful resort to sea power at all. This perhaps once prevalent attitude has long since changed, as is best evidenced by *Professor D. P. O'Connell's* able analysis, "The Influence of Law on Sea Power",[627] published in 1975. By that time UNCLOS III, the largest conference ever held under United Nations auspices, was well under way. The new LOS Convention, as the mightiest legislative undertaking ever accomplished by the international community, not only marks a triumph of law and order over chaos and lawlessness, but also considerably increased public awareness of the repercussions of the rules of law on naval practice and State responsibility. This breakthrough followed only five years after the CDDH had adopted new rules for international armed conflict at sea. The law of naval warfare is at the crossroads of these two currents of international law development: the law of the sea and the humanitarian law applicable in armed conflict.

I have tried to bring into focus here, especially for senior naval and military planners who chart defense strategies, some legal problems created by the reaffirmation and development of these two branches of the law of nations. Although there seems to be consensus that the Vienna Convention on the Law of Treaties, adopted 23 May 1969, provides the yardstick for the interpretation of Protocol I and the new LOS Convention, there are several instances where responsible opposing views or contradictory opinions are tenable. We are faced with revolutionary changes of kind, and the complexities of the interdependency of the treaty rules of Protocol I and the new LOS Convention, together with their ramifications on the law of naval warfare, require the careful attention of politicians, lawyers, diplomats, and the military.

The worst way to change a body of law is to do it inadvertently. I believe that this was the case at the CDDH regarding the treatment of the law of blockade, contraband control, submarine warfare and mine

626 London 1890.

627 Manchester 1975.

warfare. Such an accusation could not be directed against UNCLOS III, which intentionally did not touch upon any question belonging to the realm of naval warfare. However, inasmuch as the consequences from a legal point of view are concerned, there does not seem to be much difference, because the LOS Convention indirectly created similar grey zones which the CDDH had caused inadvertently.

The point in question is the unparalleled extension of the sovereignty over territorial and archipelagic waters and the inherent problems for the law of neutrality, including the aspect of self-defense in neutral waters. It cannot be a rule of law that one must wait like a "sitting duck" until the potential or real enemy delivers his first strike. This first strike might be so devastatingly forceful that the injured party could never recover. To phrase it in more concrete terms, a superpower with all probability will not run the risk of losing the better part of its nuclear armed strategic submarines because the enemy uses territorial seas or archipelagic waters of neutral States as a base for naval operations, hides his own submarines in straits used for international navigation, or abuses archipelagic waters as submarine sanctuaries.

In this context still another thorny problem may be mentioned as an example, the new rules for the protection of the natural environment. It is an eerie feeling to watch new nuclear "attack killer submarines" being launched and commissioned and at the same time to realize that the Manuals of Naval Warfare are not being revised in order to reflect the changes of law which might interfere with an attack on a nuclear powered and nuclear armed submarine, at least under certain circumstances, because of the radioactive pollution such an attack might cause. There are, of course, serious doubts whether the provisions of Protocol I will stand up to the pressures and realities of naval war. They are aggravated by the hesitation of governments who ratified Protocol I and signed the LOS Convention to face up both to the repercussions and the urgent need to rewrite the pertinent instructions and manuals.

The CDDH and UNCLOS III have opened a Pandora's box of difficulties for the rules and customs of naval warfare. It can only be hoped that the lacunae and ambiguities pointed out in this paper will not have to be ironed out by State practice, *i.e.*, by actual combat at sea. The battle should be fought with pencil and ink among those in charge of translating Protocol I and the new LOS Convention into understandable guidelines and clear advice for the seagoing officer. In doing so they will have to avoid both extremes, adopting neither the "warmonger approach" nor the overambitious and exaggerated humanitarism, in order to achieve a delicate balance of accommodation between military needs and humanitarian considerations. Assuming that the law of naval warfare and the law of neutrality in armed conflict at sea are susceptible to major changes, it is nevertheless a serious question whether this can be achieved without a new codification conference.

Western naval powers should be particularly interested in convening such a conference. As I have pointed out already they are heavily constrained by puplic opinion and a free press.[628] Any serious questions about the legality of their rules of engagement, which constitute part of the fighting instructions of their fleets, can undermine their capacity to act in times of crisis and of conflict. The rules of international law must not be ignored in the pursuit of strategic objectives, including the preservation of a global balance of deterrence.

Based upon the research reflected in this paper, I strongly hold the view that in the aftermath of the CDDH and UNCLOS III, we are desperately in need of such a codification conference, which might be best called the "United Nations Conference on the Law of Armed Conflict at Sea", or to satisfy the irreversible rule of acronyms in our penchant for abbreviation, "UNCLACS I".

---

[628] *See, supra*, 74.

MIX
Papier aus verantwortungsvollen Quellen
Paper from responsible sources
FSC® C105338

FSC
www.fsc.org

Printed by Libri Plureos GmbH
in Hamburg, Germany